INDUSTRIAL MARKETING AND SALES MANAGEMENT IN THE COMPUTER AGE

Robert F. Kelleher, President,
Advanced Industrial Marketing Systems, Inc.

CBI Publishing Company, Inc.
51 Sleeper Street
Boston, Massachusetts 02210

Copyright © 1982 by CBI Publishing Company, Inc., 51 Sleeper Street, Boston, Massachusetts 02210.

Library of Congress Cataloging in Publication Data

Kelleher, Robert F
   Industrial marketing and sales management
in the computer age.

   Bibliography: p.
   Includes index.
   1. Marketing management—Data processing.
2. Sales management—Data processing. I. Title.
HF5415.13.K39   658'.0028'54   81-10200
ISBN 0-8436-0867-6   AACR2

Printed in the United States of America

Printing (last digit): 9 8 7 6 5 4 3 2 1

Text design and composition: TKM Productions
Cover design: MaryEllen Podgorski

CONTENTS

To my family

PREFACE

Industrial Marketing and Sales Management in the Computer Age is a pioneer effort to rationalize marketing and sales management routines with help of the computer. During the more than twenty-five years the computer has been employed in industrial marketing and sales departments, application programs have been confined largely to order-filling activities, statistical sales summaries, and basic sales analysis. At present, there are no application programs involving order-getting activities in marketing and sales management at, for example, the informal level of MRP-based (material requirements planning) scheduling techniques in production and inventory management.

The uniquely productive power of the computer in industrial marketing and sales management has been ignored over the years by managers and computer specialists alike. In general, industrial marketing and sales executives do not understand the computer, and have not been taught what they need to know in order to use the computer to more effectively manage marketing and sales activities. They have not recognized, nor appreciated, the relationship between the computer, information, and marketing productivity, and they remain unaware of the computer's large potential contribution to the improvement of marketing productivity.

In many manufacturing companies selling to industrial markets, marketing and sales costs are the largest of all costs as a percentage of the sales dollar. It is therefore surprising how few marketing and sales executives would be able to provide on request an acceptable working definition of marketing productivity, let alone discuss ways the computer might be programmed to improve it. For these reasons, the rationalization of marketing and sales management routines, presented here for the first time in a book on the subject, can be thought of as representing a computer frontier in industrial operating management that has been at last crossed, explored, and mapped in a preliminary way.

Why have marketing and sales managers, and computer specialists attached no high priority to the fact that the computer is an important tool of productivity in industrial marketing and sales management applications? One explanation is that since the end of the last world war the economies of most industrialized nations have been expansionary. With sales brisk, and profits high, the subject of marketing productivity is easily ignored. But fast-growth markets of the past cannot prudently be expected to extend indefinitely into the future. A future that appears certain to include world-wide inflation, high interest rates, intense competition for dwindling raw materials resources, and a slow down of fast-growth markets, is a future also certain to challenge industry to contain costs, conserve and reallocate resources, and improve productivity. Under such circumstances, opportunities to rationalize industrial marketing and sales management routines and improve marketing productivity can no longer be overlooked.

INTRODUCTION

This book is organized into five sections designed to show the manager or computer specialist how a formal, decision-oriented, computer-based information system might be put together in industrial marketing and sales management. Part 1 traces the history of the computer in industrial management. It also points out that the operating managers who stand to benefit most from effective use of the computer have, for a variety of reasons over the years, used it least.

The computer and the bulldozer are both tools of productivity. The computer can be programmed to construct superhighways of information from mountains of data but, like the bulldozer, the computer must be directed in the "mountain-moving" tasks it is to accomplish. The computer industry has never learned, and consequently has failed to teach, that improving marketing productivity with the help of the computer depends upon the willingness and ability of managers to think about what they are trying to accomplish in different "mountain-moving" categories the computer makes possible. In order for marketing and sales managers to learn to help direct the computer in important marketing and sales management applications, there is urgent need for plain talk between managers and computer technicians.

Part 2 is a plain talk presentation of the relationship between the computer, information, and marketing productivity. Information is the product of the computer, but processed data and information are not the same thing. The right information for managers is real information, and real information is new information. New information adds to knowledge. The computer is a tool of productivity in industrial marketing and sales to the extent that real, decision-making information is made available to managers.

Part 3 is a discussion of typical productivity measurements in industry, marketing productivity analysis, and the deficiencies of custodial accounting systems in the development of accounting informa tion needed by marketing and sales managers.

Marketing productivity is defined as the sales or net profit per unit of marketing effort. It is expressed as a ratio—of sales or net profit to marketing and sales costs—for *individual products, sales territories, and customer classes.*

In the typical multiproduct manufacturing firm, single-product marketing and sales costs are not reported in an accurate, timely manner or from a managerial point of view. As a result, the following marketing "mix" misallocations are common in industrial marketing and sales:

1. Single-product marketing and sales expenditures are too large.
2. Single-product marketing and sales expenditures are too small.
3. Single-product marketing and sales expenditures are inefficiently combined.
4. The marketing "mix" is misallocated among individual products, sales territories, and customer classes.

The identification of single-product marketing and sales costs may, in the past, have exceeded the capacity of custodial accounting systems, but the computer's massive raw data manipulation capability, together with a restructuring of the Chart of Accounts, make desired information updates both possible and practical.

Part 4 is a discussion of the computer's potential contribution to improved marketing productivity. Improvement may occur through extensive analysis and manipulation of the customer list, selected marketing application programs (MAPs), and collection and analysis of vital information about marketplaces and the industries, customers, prospects, and competitors comprising them.

Part 5 is a look at the electronic future of industrial markting productivity. It examines the computer systems, advanced electronic packages, and telemetering techniques that make the paperless office possible.

While all individuals like to think they are good at what they do, the slow-growth future we envision may force reappraisal of marketing and sales management competence if manufacturing companies selling to industrial markets are to competitively survive. When a strong manufacturer develops an information system in marketing and sales management that enhances decision-making, increases operating efficiency, and improves marketing productivity, sales and profits of less informed competitors may be expected to eventually suffer. The marketing and sales manager who remains unimpressed by this inevitability is surely working on borrowed time.

Industrial marketing and sales managers have always required accurate, timely information about individual products, sales territories, and customer classes. Because such information updates were beyond the capability of manual systems in most manufacturing companies, marketing and sales executives learned a long time ago to get along without information they need. The result is that operating inefficiency and low marketing productivity are an unacknowledged way of life in industrial marketing and sales management.

This book deals with a formal, decision-oriented information system in marketing and sales management, as distinguished from a fully integrated Management Information System (MIS), because I believe the MIS concept has not lived up to early promise. Despite years of technically impressive efforts, it seems to me that the MIS, while concentrating on system integration, has tended to ignore the decision priorities of operating managers. Because I know this to be true in industrial marketing and sales management, the MIS concept is ignored in this book. Only industrial marketing and sales management activities most likely to influence marketing productivity are treated here, and these are selectively approached. I leave to others a more comprehensive presentation of industrial marketing and sales management subjects.

As a former Assistant Professor in the School of Business at a large western university, I can recommend this book as an analytical supplement to descriptive materials often used in industrial marketing and sales management courses. (I assume my readers are familiar with industrial marketing and sales management principles, the fundamentals of accounting, and managerial economics.)

Over the years of my varied experience as management student, educator, consultant to corporations, and corporate officer, I have concluded that, at top operating management levels in business organization, the interested observer finds it difficult to separate management subject from craft.

The subjects of management are many. The craft primarily involves effective decision-making capability and skills. It is to the greater perfection of the industrial marketing and sales management craft that this book is dedicated.

PART ONE

PERSPECTIVE

1

COMPUTERS IN INDUSTRIAL MARKETING AND SALES MANAGEMENT

THE INTRODUCTION OF THE COMPUTER TO MANUFACTURING COMPANIES

When the computer was first introduced to manufacturing companies over twenty-five years ago, it came in the company door and headed for the accounting department. It is easy to understand why. The computer is a vast network of electronic circuits programmed to carry out operations in logic. It is a procedure-following machine. There were well-developed, formal procedures in the accounting department that had been *manually* perfected and documented over hundreds of years by the double-entry bookkeeping systems used in accounting departments.

Programming the computer to electronically duplicate long-established manual procedures was relatively straightforward. As a consequence, computers have been successfully employed for years in accounting departments, as well as payroll, personnel, finance, and other *support* activities in manufacturing companies where satisfactory manual systems were employed before the computer came along.

The introduction of the computer to *operating* departments in manufacturing companies was a far different experience. Where written procedures existed, usually related to specific, often repetitive, routines in these departments, the computer was easily adapted. But, at decision-making levels of operating management, this was not the case.

Either manual procedures the computer could duplicate did not exist in production management and marketing and sales management, or written procedures outlined on paper did not work satisfactorily in practice. Also, informal "people" systems, apparently used in place of formal "procedure" systems in these departments, further complicated the problem. For reasons not immediately clear, reliance on informal people systems "to get the job done" was a fact of managerial life in operating departments. The procedure-following computer was stymied and, as a result, has been historically underemployed, or not employed at all, for operating management purposes in most manufacturing companies. There is a great irony to be observed here. In manufacturing companies, operating managers who can potentially benefit most from effective use of the computer have, for a variety of reasons over the years, employed it least.

PRODUCTIVITY AND THE MARGINAL VALUE OF INFORMATION PRODUCED BY COMPUTERS

The nature of information for operating management purposes will be discussed in Chapter 3. For now, attention is focused on the fact that the marginal value of information produced by computers is not the same in all departments of manufacturing companies.

1. In the accounting department, as discussed, the transfer of a satisfactory manual system to the computer has been straightforward. At the same time, *there is comparatively little computer payoff in terms of increased accounting efficiency and improved productivity*. It seems that, long before the computer, most of the important custodial accounting questions had been asked, and logical procedures were established to develop accurate, timely information in answer to these questions. So, from the point of view of the accounting manager, the marginal value of accounting information produced by a computer system, when compared to a satisfactory manual system, is *small*.

2. In production management, getting a computer-based information system to work effectively has been complicated by the absence of satisfactory manual systems. There have been many false starts as a result, and much disappointment. Looking back, it took many years (the mid-1960's) before the computer found a place as an operating management tool in production departments. The effectiveness of the computer in production management was only real-

ized when production managers, systems analysts, and computer programmers, frustrated by lack of success with the computer and searching for answers, began asking operating questions no one apparently had asked before in production departments.

When computer programs were written providing accurate, timely information in answer to some of these questions, *a comparatively big computer payoff in terms of increased operating efficiency and improved plant productivity resulted.* From the point of view of the production manager, the marginal value of production information provided by a formal, decision-oriented computer system, when compared to unsatisfactory or nonexistent manual systems, is *large.* Some of these operating questions, and computer-based MRP (material requirements planning) scheduling techniques in production and inventory management, will be discussed in Chapter 4.

3.   In industrial marketing and sales management there is also an absence of satisfactory manual systems. But, while we are able to discuss in Chapter 4 the contribution to plant productivity made by the computer and MRP, no equivalent success story can be told in marketing and sales. If the computer serves marketing and sales management at all, it serves without distinction. If production departments prior to the development of MRP were informal people systems mired in the inefficiency of *ad hoc* expediting routines "to get the job done," that claim can also be made with regard to many marketing and sales activities.

Learning to ask important operating questions no one apparently has asked before in marketing and sales departments, and rethinking marketing and sales management functions to accommodate the procedure-following demands of the computer, are possible and long overdue. When computer programs are written providing accurate, timely information in answer to some of these questions, *the biggest computer payoff of all departments in terms of increased efficiency and improved marketing productivity can be realized.* From the point of view of marketing and sales managers, the marginal value of marketing and sales information provided by a formal, decision-oriented computer system, when compared to unsatisfactory or nonexistent manual systems, is *very large.*

The discussion thus far has centered around the value of the computer in terms of the contribution information can make to productivity in various departments of manufacturing companies. We have concluded that a very large contribution to marketing productivity can be made by formal, decision-oriented, information systems in marketing and sales management. Yet, it is fair to say that the computer, as a tool of productivity, has been least used by marketing and sales managers. The question, of course, is why.

A ROADBLOCK TO MARKETING PRODUCTIVITY

The aim of this book is to educate marketing and sales executives in manufacturing companies to become involved in getting more effective computing done in their departments. Formal, decision-oriented, information systems in marketing and sales management will greatly increase operating efficiencies by eliminating dependency on informal people systems. But, while marketing and sales managers must be part of the design and development of such systems, chances are the typical industrial marketing and sales manager is uncomfortable around computers.

To most of us on the outside looking in, computers are awesome. We are intimidated by them, and wish we could better understand them. Although we can see the computer we cannot see what is happening inside it. What is happening inside the computer is, by its nature, invisible to us.

We wonder about invisible forces. We ask a few questions, and read a few articles, but computer technology is complicated. Getting to know the jargon is a task in itself, and early enthusiasm turns cold. The more we learn, the less we seem to understand. We feel there are probably better uses for the computer in marketing and sales management, but we do not know what they are. No one else seems to know either. With nowhere to turn, our apprehensions about computers are compounded.

Our uneasiness results in strange behavior. Some managers, aware of the computer's expense and the proliferation of useless computer print-outs gathering on their desks, disapprovingly shake their heads while maintaining a discreet, nonmanagerial silence. Others seek refuge in a pretense of computer knowledge and enthusiasm, hoping not to be discovered. Still others try to ignore the computer, ostrich-like, with the wish that their feelings of inaptitude, and the computer, will fade away together. But the feelings remain, as the computer remains.

Computer specialists have been small help in this regard over the years. Trained in the standard application programs associated with marketing and sales activities in manufacturing companies, they have failed to explain effective use of the computer to industrial marketing and sales managers, or where the greatest potential computer payoffs in marketing and sales management applications may be. While computers have been available for use in industrial marketing and sales departments for many years, two facts are undeniable:

1. Most industrial marketing and sales managers do not understand the computer, and have not been taught what they need to know in order to more effectively use the computer in their departments. They do not sufficently understand the concept of marketing productivity, and are unaware of the computer's large potential contribution to the improvement of marketing productivity.
2. No tool of productivity remotely resembling computer-based MRP scheduling techniques in production and inventory management exists in industrial marketing and sales management. Yet, most companies with production departments also have marketing and sales departments, and, as already suggested, total marketing and sales costs as a percentage of the sales dollar may be the largest of all costs in many manufacturing companies.

Clearly, something is wrong. Somewhere during the past twenty-five years an important turn in the road was missed. Marketing and sales managers, uncomfortable around computers, either underemploy them, or do not use them at all, in important industrial marketing and sales management applications. The result is a roadblock to marketing productivity. To help clear the roadblock, and to learn to appreciate the potential of the computer as a tool of marketing productivity, we need to retrace steps and try to learn what happened.

A Transforming Invention

If the computer is not humanity's most important invention, it is certain to be viewed by historians on the scale of the printing press, steam engine, automobile, and airplane. Along with the computer, these major inventions have significantly and permanently altered or transformed environments in which they have been used.

While we may fault the computer industry for failure to explain the most productive uses of the computer in industrial marketing and sales management applications, it is true that, as the computer has been used, the range of its applications has expanded. Some of the most productive computer applications in industrial marketing and sales management have only gradually been realized and defined. At the beginning, neither computer specialists nor marketing and sales managers could possibly have known the full range of applications for this transforming invention. As an example, it has taken years for the relationship between the computer, information, and marketing productivity to be recognized and appreciated. While a more user-oriented technical elite may have speeded the computer's progress as a tool of productivity in industrial marketing and sales management applications, it is probable that years of trial-and-error experimentation would have been required to reach present understanding anyway.

It must also be noted that printers guide printing presses, gaining experience with printing in the process. The same observation applies to engineers with steam engines, drivers with automobiles, and pilots with airplanes. But the computer, in marketing and sales applications, is not guided by marketing and sales managers. Once programmed, the computer operates automatically. The control mechanism is inside the computer.

Technicians closest to the computer usually understand little about marketing and sales management. The manager closest to marketing and sales management problems typically understands little about the computer. The technician and the manager speak different languages with respect to what they are trying to accomplish, and the result has been a computer stalemate in industrial marketing and sales management.

The stalemate has been prolonged because people in management, being in positions they may wish to protect, only reluctantly admit ignorance of a subject they are presumed to know. When the subject is as large and pervasive as the computer, pretense can become a political way of life. Buzz words and jargon try to pass for knowledge and inquiry. The truth, having become inconvenient, disappears.

□ The truth is computer applications in industrial marketing and sales management are unimpressive, and fall far short of a contribution to the improvement of marketing productivity.

□ The truth is technical trivia in increased doses is precisely what marketing and sales managers do not need.

□ The truth is the computer industry has never learned, and consequently has failed to teach, that effective use of the computer in industrial marketing and sales depends upon the willingness of managers to think differently about what they try to accomplish as managers.

□ The truth is the underemployment of the computer in marketing and sales management will continue unless effective use of this tool of productivity is explained to marketing and sales managers in plain talk. Plain talk and a common language between technicians and managers are what have been missing all these years.

THE COMPUTER AND THE BULLDOZER

For operating management purposes, the computer can be explained in simple, nontechnical terms. Computers, and what computers can be programmed to accomplish, need plain talk and easily understood explanations if they are to be productively employed in industrial marketing and sales management applications.

While marketing and sales managers need to know little about the computer as a machine, they need to understand the computer as a transforming invention, and to be aware that this transforming capability requires willingness on their parts to rethink what they are trying to accomplish as managers. Toward this end, a comparison of the computer and the bulldozer is revealing.

The computer and the bulldozer are transforming inventions that seem unrelated. But, for our purposes, they have much in common. Both are inventions helping people accomplish things previously considered impossible or impractical. The bulldozer extends muscle power. The computer extends mental power. In both instances, however, the power extensions are specific and limited

Bulldozers, for example, do not design superhighways. They make construction of superhighways practical, though, by moving dirt around faster and more efficiently than ever before. Computers, contrary to myth, do not solve problems. However, they make many problem-solving projects practical for the first time by moving data around faster and more efficiently than ever before. The computer and the bulldozer transform environments. It is the way in which they alter environments that describes their most important common feature—properly used, both machines greatly improve productivity.

Suppose we all live in town A (Figure 1.1), and commute to work in a factory located at B, twenty miles away as the crow flies. In this example, the crow has to fly over densely forested, mountainous terrain. Long ago, a road was built around one side of this mountain range. We have grown accustomed to this road because we drive over it twice a day when we work, about thirty-two miles each way. The two-hour round trip represents lost time. Commuters do no productive work while they drive, and most people agree there are better, more productive leisure activities than commuting by car to work.

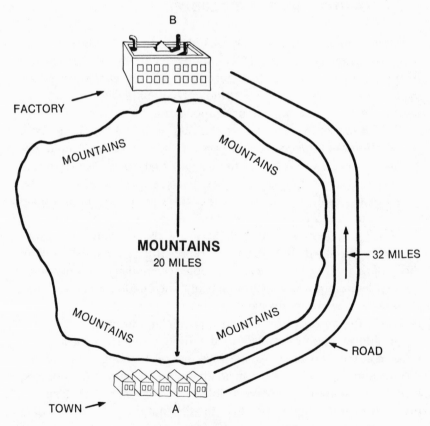

FIGURE 1.1
Getting to Work—Before the Bulldozer

Before the invention of the bulldozer, the issue of unproductive commute time in our example was not likely to be seriously discussed. Nothing that would make an important difference, in either time spent or distance traveled, could be done anyway. Moving the town to the factory, or the factory to the town, was impossible. Cutting a highway through the mountains with picks and shovels, although possible, was impractical. The money to pay armies of workers for the years required to complete the project would be exorbitant and, considering the forest and the twenty-mile mountain range, most of the commuters would be dead, or the factory closed, by the time the new road was completed anyway. Because it was impractical to think about the advantages of a superhighway cut through the mountains, commuters learned to put up with inconvenience and, on their way to and from work, thought about other things.

After the invention of the bulldozer, unproductive commute time in our example often became an issue. Commuters had choices about roads traveled to commute to work. Bulldozers and other earth-moving equipment could quickly and efficiently move tons of dirt and rock so that superhighways could be built where once impassable mountains had been. Construction costs still had to be weighed against benefits to be realized but, criteria met and the construction decision made, projects that were once considered impossible or impractical could be undertaken. In the planning stages of projects today, construction engineers may consider the advantages of moving mountains. In our example, construction engineers, thinking in "mountain-moving" categories made possible by the bulldozer, would soon have a superhighway built where impassable mountains had been.

Time spent commuting to work would be reduced from two hours to forty minutes. Miles driven would decrease nearly 40 percent (Figure 1.2). But we do not require an example to convince us that society has endorsed the improved social productivity made possible by well-placed superhighways. All we need to do is look around us.

It is easy to see a mountain of dirt and rock. Even when we cannot measure it with our eyes, we can sense its obstructing presence in the long road we must drive to get around it. It is easy to think about moving mountains we can see. Marketing and sales landscapes are mountainous terrain also. The mountains are data. Marketing and sales managers cannot "see" mountains of data surrounding them, but have grown accustomed over the years to traveling long roads in

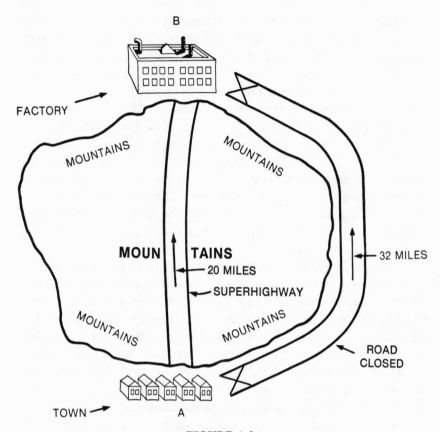

FIGURE 1.2
Getting to Work—After the Bulldozer

the same unconscious way as the commuters in our example. To the marketing and sales managers who are unaware of the existence of these obstructions to efficiency and progress, the long roads are the only roads.

The computer, like the bulldozer, moves mountains. The computer can be programmed to move mountains of data faster, more accurately, and more efficiently than ever before. But, like the bulldozer, the computer must be directed in the "mountain-moving" tasks it is to accomplish. No matter what other competence computer specialists or marketing and sales managers possess, they must learn to think in different, "mountain-moving" categories about marketing and sales management activities if the productivity of marketing and sales departments is to be improved.

Construction engineers, thinking in "mountain-moving" categories made possible by the bulldozer, design high-speed superhighways that improve social productivity. In much the same way, marketing and sales managers, systems analysts, and computer programmers, thinking in "mountain-moving" categories made possible by the computer, will design information superhighways that improve marketing productivity.

LEARNING TO THINK IN MOUNTAIN-MOVING CATEGORIES

Learning to think about industrial marketing and sales management activities in "mountain-moving" categories made possible by the computer is the important turn in the road missed by computer specialists and managers long ago. It is also one of the reasons this book has been written. It is as though, following the invention of the bulldozer, commuters and construction engineers remained unaware, or indifferent to the fact, that a new road cut through mountainous terrain might be socially desirable. Using the computer to improve marketing productivity has, unfortunately, been ignored in the same way.

We have already suggested that fast-growth markets of the past, while covering a multitude of sins, cannot prudently be expected to indefinitely extend into the future. Industrial marketing and sales managers need formal, decision-oriented, information systems now. Willingness to rethink what they are trying to accomplish as managers is a prerequisite for that accomplishment.

The case for formal, decision-oriented, information systems in industrial marketing and sales is best made by the time-perishability of data for operating management purposes. Marketing and sales managers have always needed accurate, timely information to manage efficiently. Because such updates were beyond the capability of manual systems, managers have learned to put up with inefficiency. This subject is discussed in Chapter 3.

Learning to think in different "mountain-moving" categories about marketing and sales management activities demands managerial imagination. Sometimes we are frustrated trying to see with our eyes what can only be seen with our imaginations. The computer is a good example of this. We employ imaginative vision to understand the computer for operating management purposes in Chapter 2.

Marketing expenditures and marketing and sales effort are allocated by managers to products, sales territories, and customer classes. We close this chapter with a few examples of what may be accomplished when marketing and sales managers, and computer specialists, learn to think in different "mountain-moving" categories about products, sales territories, and customer classes:

1. *Products.* Most contemporary manufacturing companies market and sell multiproduct lines. While custodial accounting systems typically report single-product *manufacturing* costs, single-product *marketing and sales* costs are not reported. All products contribute to net profit, after marketing and sales costs, at different rates. Some products may negatively contribute to net profit. If dollars of marketing and sales effort were reallocated among individual products, net profit could be increased. Single-product *marketing and sales* costs can be made available to managers as a consequence of the computer's massive raw data manipulation capability. We discuss this subject in Chapter 6.

2. *Sales territories.* A fully staffed manufacturer, working with manufacturers' reps, might employ forty rep firms and offices to represent the manufacturers' products in twenty major, and twenty satellite, markets in the United States. Within these forty sales territories are over one hundred sales areas assigned to individual rep salespersons. It is unlikely that marketing and sales managers responsible for results obtained by reps would, in the absence of formal, decision-oriented, information systems, have the information updates about sales territories and sales areas that improved productivity requires.

As one example of vital information a computer can be programmed to provide for marketing and sales managers working with reps see MAP CF-3A in selected marketing application programs (MAPs) presented in Chapter 8.

3. *Customer classes.* Most manufacturers list customers, but marketing and sales executives can employ customer lists to greatly expand the range of useful information they have about customers and prospects. The computer can be programmed to provide the following updated information about customers:

> name
> bill-to address by city, zip code, county, state
> ship-to address by city, zip code, county, state
> purchase contact

use contact
SIC
rep code
establishment size code
sales revenue code
model number or application code.
The care and feeding of the customer list is discussed in Chapter 7.

Learning to think about industrial marketing and sales management activities in different, ''mountain-moving'' categories the computer makes possible is a prerequisite to design and development of the MAPs required in order to increase operating efficiency and improve marketing productivity. The computer's payoff in industrial marketing and sales management is realized at the level of such marketing application programs.

PART TWO

COMPUTERS, INFORMATION, AND MARKETING PRODUCTIVITY

2

PLAIN TALK ABOUT COMPUTERS

Marketing and sales executives do not need to become involved with the complexities of the computer as a machine. Because the computer's payoff in industrial marketing and sales management is at the level of marketing application programs (MAPs), the time and effort spent by managers working with the computer should be directed toward the creation of MAPs they will need to penetrate markets at high productivity levels. Understanding computer hardware, software, and technical trivia in great detail is no substitute for knowledge about application programs, their design, development, and informational use.

To guide and assist computer programmers, marketing and sales managers need to understand what the computer is and does and how the computer can be used to improve marketing productivity. They also need to understand the unique nature of information the computer can be programmed to produce. This chapter presents an overview of the computer, and Chapter 3 discusses information and productivity.

A COMPUTER OVERVIEW

The design and development of the MAPs we are discussing involve dialogue between managers and computer programmers. The programmer is a computer specialist who can ordinarily be counted on to know little about the important MAPs a manager may require. Typically, the programmer has no industrial marketing and sales management background, and so cannot be expected to understand the range of marketing and sales management problems.

Because computer programmers can complicate the development of an application program if they choose, it is common sense to make them as comfortable as possible by demonstrating an interest in their subject. Also, because the amount of information a good application program can provide is finite, there is an infinity of information we are unable to produce. There are more questions we cannot ask than we can ask, so we save time and avoid frustration (our own and the programmer's) by knowing our system's capabilities and limitations.

Developing Imaginative Vision

Nothing complicates learning what we need to know about the computer more than its invisibility. We can see the computer, but what the computer does is invisible to us. The space inside the computer, and the speed at which the computer travels across the space, can be thought of as representing an electronic universe. We have difficulty adjusting our minds to comprehend the computer's electronic universe in the same way we have difficulty adjusting our minds to comprehend like phenomena in the physical universe. The problem is that we are trying to see with our eyes what can only be seen with our imaginations. To understand what the computer does, and how the computer can be used in the design and development of MAPs, we need to close our eyes and try to imagine:

1. *The computer's space.* We can easily imagine a file cabinet. We see and may use many of them every day. We slide a drawer open and locate, by alphabetical file section, the document we are after. The system is imperfect, however. If the file is full, we may have to go to a continuation file where our search begins again. If what we are looking for is not to be found there either, perhaps someone has removed it. Is there a signature on the OUT card?

If we were trying to imagine a perfect filing system, what would it be? Endless space, perhaps, so we'd never waste time hunting through continuation files again. And, for our purposes, file space is what the computer makes possible. The computer's space is the apparently endless, electronic filing system we have imagined.

2. *The computer's total recall capability.* We can use our imaginations to envision a fingertip file system control button that imme-

diately and unerringly retrieves items we put into our apparently endless file. If there were such a button, no more time would be wasted chasing after signatures on OUT cards.

For our purposes, the computer has the total recall capability of the fingertip file system control button we have imagined. It knows the location of every item it has filed away for us, and can swiftly and accurately retrieve items we instruct it to retrieve. It can perform various operations in logic involving the items, and then return the items to the apparently endless file, all in accordance with procedures we have specified that it follow.

3.   *The computer's speed.*   If the apparently endless electronic filing space we have imagined were only traversable at the speed of the fastest file clerk, we would spend most of the time we are involved with file data waiting for a particular item to be retrieved. But, as we know, the computer is fast. To appreciate the computer's speed, we need to try to see with our imaginations again.

We can easily imagine a typewriter. We have seen many of them, and may use one ourselves from time to time. If we type at the rate of sixty words a minute, and if the average word we type is six characters long including spaces, we depress typewriter keys an average of six times a second, or a single typewriter key every .166 of a second.

Now we have to be careful to say here that computer speeds vary. The fastest computer at present would perform well above the computer in our example. The computer we refer to operates at relatively modest speed. Still, in .166 of a second, the average time it takes in our example to depress a single typewriter key, the computer can add over 50,000 pairs of digits. By the time we have completed typing sixty words at the rate we have been imagining, the computer has completed over 18 million of these two-digit additions.

Computer operations are timed in nanoseconds (billionths of a second). You can get a sense of the magnitude a billion represents by figuring out how old you'll be 31.7 years from now. That will be when the next billion seconds pass by. The time delay of some computer circuits is twenty nanoseconds. Get your imagination working on the following relationship: Twenty nanoseconds are to a second as twenty seconds are to 31.7 years.

The additions we are discussing have other uses than summing digits for the sake of an arithmetic answer. A little later, when we discuss the computer's capability to carry out operations in logic, the impact of nanosecond speed proficiency will be more fully realized.

4. *The computer's massive raw data manipulation capability.* Most of us who work in the marketing and sales departments of manufacturing companies have:

A number of products for sale, rent, or lease

A number of pre-sale quotations involving these products

A number of sales made as a consequence of quotations won

A number of product specifications, types, and sizes

A number of list prices for products, discount schedules, and quantity prices

A number of product applications

A number of customers, classifiable by geographic location, industry, establishment type, establishment size, product application, and sales revenue share

A number of salespersons, classifiable by geographic location, distributor or rep type and size, customer type and size, prospect type and size, product application, sales revenue share by customer, and sales revenue expectation by prospect

A number of prospects, classifiable by geographic location, industry, establishment type, establishment size, product application, and sales revenue expectation.

There are a great number of "sorting" possibilities indicated by this short summary. Not all are equally useful to managers but, by listing some of the many sorting possibilities that may interest us, we can appreciate the quantities of data we may need to have manipulated in order to produce the decision-making information we seek.

We have found it is possible to feel more comfortable around the computer when we understand that its reputation as a massive manipulator of raw data gives managers an information-producing capability not available manually, and that this well-deserved reputation is the product of the computer's apparently endless file space, incredible speed, and total recall capability. Without the need to mention bits, bytes, and buses, or binary, octal, and hexidecimal number systems, by using plain talk and our imaginations, we are now familiar with:

1. *The computer's space.* For our purposes, it is an apparently endless electronic filing system.

2. *The computer's total recall capability.* It knows the location of every item it has filed away for us, and can swiftly and

accurately retrieve the items we instruct it to retrieve. It can perform various operations in logic involving the items, and return the items to the apparently endless file, all according to procedures we specify.

3. *The computer's speed.* For our purposes, we can say that the computer travels at nearly the speed of light.

4. *The computer's massive raw data manipulation capability.* The combination of file capacity, accurate total recall, and "speed of light" calculations gives managers an information-producing capability not otherwise available to them.

It was mentioned in Chapter 1 that the computer is a vast network of electronic circuits programmed to carry out operations in logic. In addition to what we have already learned in our discussion about the computer, when we understand the nature of these "operations in logic" we will have come a long way toward understanding the use of the computer as a tool of productivity in industrial marketing and sales management.

Operations in Logic

We have presented an overview of what the computer *is* in simple, nontechnical terms. What the computer *does*, in order to produce from raw data manipulations the decision-making information of interest to us as marketing and sales managers, can also be explained in simple, nontechnical, terms. But we need to use our imaginations again.

Figure 2.1 represents a two-switch electrical circuit similar to the one that operates the car radio. Because we do not want the radio left playing when we are not in the car, we have developed an electrical circuit requiring that the ignition switch and radio switch both have to be in the ON position if power is to reach the radio. If either switch is in the OFF position, the radio cannot play.

This exercise of our imaginations comes in two parts. The first part involves picturing in our minds the two-switch electrical circuit we have sketched, and realizing that the computer is a collection of large numbers of such circuits interconnected. The second part involves imagining, superimposed on these circuits for use by the computer, certain syllogistic constructions that can be employed to process data and create information. This second part is the ingeniously applied, direct result of humanity's ancient preoccupation with the ability to logically reason.

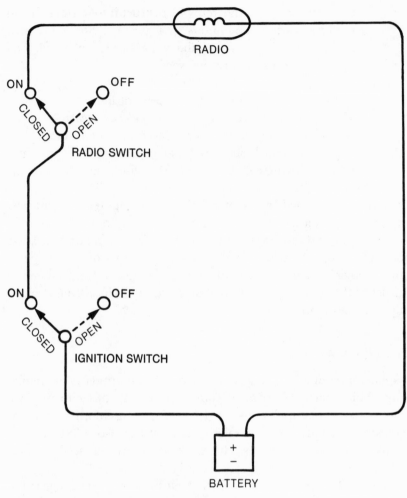

FIGURE 2.1
A Car Radio Circuit

The subject of logic is old, large, and well beyond the scope of this book. But we need not be students of logic to understand the use to which a logical process has been put. When we understand how basic syllogistic reasoning is employed in computing, and the power of elementary logic circuits when correctly programmed and combined in large numbers, we will understand in general how the computer processes data to create information. A deductive reasoning method, the syllogism formalizes the reasoning process that permits conclusions to be reached about premises made, in accordance with the rules of good logic. When premises are true, and the conclusion regarding the premises logically derived, the syllogism adds to what we know by the process of inference.

In Figure 2.2, we have substituted, for the ignition switch and radio switch in Figure 2.1, Premise 1 and Premise 2, respectively. The radio has been replaced with a Conclusion. Following the rules of good logic, we are able to infer as follows:

Premise 1: All A is B.
Premise 2: All B is C.
Conclusion: Therefore, all A is C.

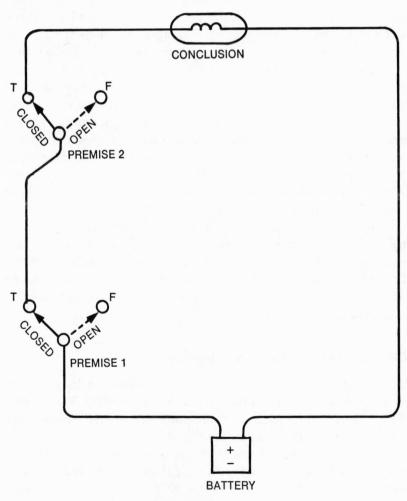

FIGURE 2.2
A Computer Logic Circuit

This is an example of an AND circuit. If Premise 1 is true AND Premise 2 is true, the Conclusion reached is true. AND circuits, together with OR and NOT circuits, represent three ways computers can be programmed at the level of elementary logic circuits to perform operations in logic and produce information.

In Premise 1, we already know that all A is B. By the time a Conclusion has been reached, we have learned that all A is C also. Whether learning that all A is also C is important does not concern us at this time. We are trying at the moment to make clear that, if information is to be generated with the help of the computer, it is generated in this manner.

We are able to logically deal with things that have one of only two conditions, or states. These might be *Yes* or *No, True* or False, *Go* or *No Go, Open* or *Closed,* or *On* or *Off.* No other conditions or states are possible. When you think about it, there are many situations with which we deal every day that are not describable using only two categories. But there are also many conditions or states that we are able to classify in this way. One is thus able to program or arrange computer circuits so that elementary logical conclusions can be reached and inferences made. By putting a large number of these elementary logic circuits together correctly, so that the output of one is the input to another, the computer's space, speed, and accuracy may be employed to manipulate raw data in ways that would be impossible or impractical to duplicate manually.

For marketing and sales managers, and other operating managers in industry, this awesome capability can be used to produce essential management information never before available to them. The computer is a tool of productivity for operating managers to the extent that important, previously unavailable, decision-making information can be generated.

The Computer as Problem Solver and Decision Maker

It was inevitable that a mythology would develop to help people explain the deep mysteries of the computer to themselves. We are now able to debunk two prominent computer myths, and increase our understanding of the computer at the same time.

Elementary logic circuits in the computer, employing *High* or *Low* voltage to activate the logic rather than switches as depicted in our illustrations, conduct electrical signals as technicians have programmed them to do. The computer does not know what is being done with the signals its circuits conduct, so the computer does no thinking. It is analysts and programmers who do all the thinking, logical or illogical. The blindly obedient computer follows directions. Blaming a computer for not providing information that is needed is like blaming a high-speed sportscar for allowing itself to be driven into a ditch.

To accept the myth that the computer solves problems not only blurs the facts, but it also creates an obstacle to being able to feel comfortable around the computer. Any problem the computer provides information to solve was pre-solved by programmers who developed the necessary sequential operations in logic. Although answers vary with data inputs, the step-by-step procedures the computer follows do not vary within the structure of a particular program. If the program does what it was intended to do, these steps and procedures are always the same. We are the problem solvers. The computer is a machine we use to process answers to the problems we have solved.

To accept the myth that the computer makes decisions blurs facts as well. We are the decision-makers. Within limits imposed by logical reasoning, the computer can be programmed to select among a number of decision alternatives. But this is a limited capability that needs to be clearly understood. Management decisions are not always based on logic, and the computer has no intuition and no emotion. The decision-making capability of the computer, when logically based, is in the hands of the people who use it. We are able to feel more comfortable around the computer when we realize that the true problem-solvers and decision-makers are ourselves.

AN IDEAL COMPUTER SYSTEM

This book is concerned with the computer and computer programming only to the extent that knowledge of these subjects is required by marketing and sales executives in the development of MAPs they will need to increase operating efficiency and improve marketing productivity. Discussion regarding specific kinds of computer equipment and system components would fill many volumes and is beyond the scope of this book. Nevertheless, because the choice of a computer system can in itself influence solutions to management problems, or extend and complicate the problems to be solved, a few comments are appropriate regarding an ideal computer system for operating management applications in most manufacturing companies.

Computers can be programmed to do many things. Marketing and sales managers in industry need massive raw data manipulations to produce decision-making information. These massive manipulations of raw data will be required for updating purposes on a regular, perhaps daily, basis. Perhaps you will recall when data was stored on punched cards, placed in metal trays, and then put away on shelves. This data storage method did not encourage the massive raw data manipulations that convert data to useful information. Difficulty in combining data discouraged flexibility in this regard. With the introduction of magnetic tape, serial processing of data could take place at much faster speeds than had been possible before magnetic tape. There was still only one program to each data file, however, so there remained a limit to the data that could be combined.

When magnetic disks and drums were introduced to computing, it became possible to randomly access files, search for and sort out data, and combine data from different files without having to also process irrelevant data. Random access capability is a basic feature of the ideal computer system for industrial marketing and sales managers.

While magnetic disks and drums made random access to files possible, the labeling of data in the computer's memory introduced the concept of "data base" to computing. With older data management methods, individual departments in a company are expected to organize their own file records to suit particular information needs. This results in duplication of data from one department to another, and in redundance in data and in the overhead cost-related to file creation, organizing, maintenance, and updating. Data base management is an important feature of the ideal computer system we are describing.

Data base management eliminates data redundance while optimizing file access and economy. The problems introduced by storing the same data in different files, and by different update levels of the same data in different files, are removed. By eliminating the potential for error associated with having the same data stored and maintained in more than one place, a new level of file integrity is introduced. The importance of high-level file integrity, made possible by new file management software aspects of the data base concept, cannot be overemphasized. It is another feature of the ideal computer system in industrial operating management.

Data that may be referenced and updated daily for management purposes must be correct. The effectiveness of the entire system is a function of data quality. The quality of system files is reflected in the accuracy, updating level, and general accessibility of data stored in the files. This is all the more true, and desirable, when an integrated data base common to all departments serves for the processing of a wide variety of applications.

The objective of any computer-based information system should be to generate important information accurately, quickly, economically, and in an appropriate form. There is no greater assurance that these objectives will be met than putting the computer into the hands of users, with data entered by users as it happens, at CRT (cathode-ray tube) terminals. Thanks to microprocessor technology, higher data transmission teleprocessing speeds, new support software, and a variety of input/output terminals for data collection, visual display, and report printing, users communicating with the computer at suitably located CRT terminals in the office and plant are an increasingly common sight. They represent another important feature of the ideal computer system for operating managers in most manufacturing companies.

To summarize, some of the basic features of an ideal computer system for operating managers are:

1. Random access to data files
2. Accurate and timely data gathered into a single integrated data base common to all departments
3. Data base management
4. High file integrity
5. The people responsible for doing the work are also responsible for entering the day's data into the computer
6. Application programs to answer important operating questions
7. Visual display and print available for on-the-spot inquiry and information in support of more enlightened management decision-making.

A Look at Costs

Computer costs are variable. There are as many different price schedules as there are systems and components available, and that would make a long list. It is expected that rapid advances in computer technology will be accompanied by sharply reduced unit computing costs in the future, though, and that development is worth keeping a finger on. We see these anticipated cost-performance relationships as firm support for what we have said about formal, decision-oriented computer-based information systems in industrial marketing and sales management.

For example, it is expected that during the coming years, with electronic circuits operating in faster switching speed ranges, computer processing costs will cease being a constraint in most applications. Economies are also to be realized as a consequence of new storage methods and techniques associated with bubble memories, microfiche, thin-film magnetics, and video-disks.

In Chapter 10, we discuss the impact on marketing productivity of transmission media which make possible the regular use of voiced, still-image, and video-displayed data for more efficient communication. Satellites, fiberoptics, mobile radio, and microwave technologies are expected to make these new electronic transmission methods economically feasible. The unit costs of input/output terminals may also be anticipated to sharply decrease during the 1980s as forms of speech processing, laser optic and ink-jet printing, soft displays, and automated electronic controls become as commonly used as telephones, copiers, CRT's, and typewriters are today.

Also, as computer-based information systems continue to be designed around the needs of the people who use them, the unit cost of software is expected to be reduced. This will take the form of prepackaged programs and new programming techniques, which will make it possible for lay persons to modify their systems and, to some extent, actually do some programming of their own.

As previously stated, marketing and sales executives who believe formal, decision-oriented, information systems are not an inevitable part of industrial marketing and sales management in the future are working on borrowed time. The economics we have been discussing seem to support such a conclusion.

In closing this chapter of plain talk about computers, it is important to emphasize that the computer has matured in its role as a tool for managers. ' Bread and butter'' applications have long been with us. Application programs that involve keeping the company's books, billing customers, and paying employees and suppliers are directed to important, procedural parts of business which will, of course, continue. But new application programs, many involving areas of management previously ignored, may be expected to join them. The computer can be programmed to provide management intelligence in the form of important, once unavailable, information to enhance decision-making.

Once such information is obtained, it may be dynamically used by those who direct business operations, to the competitive advantage of the company rather than simple record-keeping after the fact. It is by use of such information that industrial marketing and sales managers will increase operating efficiency and improve marketing productivity.

There is an old computer story that says when managers ask for a cup of information, computer people turn a hose on them. As already mentioned, all information is not equally useful to managers. What is information anyway? And how do we know the kind of information we are getting is the kind of information we need? Is there a particular kind of information that helps improve productivity? These questions are discussed in Chapter 3.

3
INFORMATION AND MARKETING PRODUCTIVITY

Efficiency is a static concept. The concept of marketing productivity, compared to efficiency, is dynamic in the sense that it refers to a generative source of *continuing* activity. We learn in the present chapter that the generative source of *continuing* activity in industrial marketing and sales management is a decision-making capability enhanced by real information.

The last chapter concluded with an old computer story that says when managers ask for a cup of information, computer people turn a hose on them. The story supports a claim made in this book: Industrial marketing and sales managers in most manufacturing companies do not understand the nature of information they require in order to improve marketing productivity—neither do computer programmers. So computer people do what they know best. They process data, and the more the better. Computer paper manufacturers prosper because information quantity, presumed to be understood by everyone, is used in place of information quality, in this case understood by few. More information is not what is needed in industrial marketing and sales management.

As Chapter 1 stated, the value of the computer in various departments of manufacturing companies can be explained in terms of the contribution information can make to productivity. It has taken years for the relationship between the computer, information, and marketing productivity to be recognized and appreciated—and the recognition and appreciation are not presently widespread. In this chapter, we discuss information and marketing productivity in some detail, in order that the circle of recognition and appreciation may be widened.

WHAT IS INFORMATION ANYWAY?

There are a number of ways information is defined in any good dictionary. Two definitions are of interest here. The first definition relates to computer technology. Information, in the computer world, is "any data that can be coded for processing by a computer or similar device." While this may be a useful definition for computer specialists, it does not adequately define information for industrial marketing and sales management purposes. According to the second definition, information is "any knowledge *gained* through communication, research, instruction, etc." *Gained* is the operative word. This definition of information is appropriate to the marketing and sales management task. It is fair to say that these two definitions of information are not distinguished in most manufacturing companies by marketing and sales managers, or computer programmers.

To computer specialists, information tends to be data processed by the computer. They are usually ready to admit that all information is not equally useful to operating managers, but they are apt to be the wrong people to consult when asking, "How do we know that the kind of information we get is the kind of information we need?"

Information is the product of the computer. However, for operating management purposes, data that is processed, and information, are not the same thing. The information required by marketing and sales managers, in order to increase operating efficiency and improve marketing productivity, is not the automatic consequence of data processing.

Increasing operating efficiency in a manufacturing firm is like finding gold buried under your house. The discovery of buried treasure in a place where you have lived many years depends as much on right information as the right prospecting or mining techniques.

Marketing and sales managers will increase operating efficiency, and improve marketing productivity, when right information is made available to them. The right information for industrial marketing and sales management is real information. Real information is new information. Discovering gold buried under the house requires new information. If the information about the gold were already known, it would already have been discovered. Information that reaffirms old facts, what is already known, is not real information. It is apparent information. Computer applications in industrial marketing and sales management mostly produce apparent information. It is not difficult to understand why.

Apparent information is in plentiful supply, and can be comfortably reassuring. Real information is relatively scarce, can be difficult to get, and profoundly disquieting. Because real information provides insight into what has not been known, its presence can put an end to the pleasure of basking in reflected glories.

Real information requires that questions be asked that may challenge old assumptions. But if marketing and sales managers have not been taught to understand the nature of the information they require in order to manage efficiently, they can hardly be expected to understand the kind of questions they should be asking. To ask important operating questions that encourage the development of real information, these managers need to learn to think about what they are trying to accomplish in different categories the computer makes possible. As discussed in Chapter 1, they have not been taught to understand the computer in this way.

The information we are discussing may be classified in a number of ways. Information may be primary, secondary, internal, or external, but real information contributes to our knowledge about a subject. Real information is knowledge *gained*. The only way to acquire *more* knowledge is to add *new* knowledge to *old* knowledge. Information theory is a big subject, and "What is information anyway?" a big question. Still, within the context of information needs in industrial marketing and sales management, it is correct to conclude that real information and apparent information are not the same. We note with interest that in most manufacturing companies the present use of the computer in marketing and sales management applications makes no sharp distinction in this regard.

DATA, INFORMATION, KNOWLEDGE

A good way to understand information is to understand where it comes from, where real information can lead to, and what constitutes useful information for marketing and sales managers interested in a systematic approach to the improvement of marketing productivity. Marketing and sales executives are paid to make decisions that help assure the competitive future of a company. Effective decisions are the consequence of an intricate process that may involve fact-gathering, measurement, analysis, interpretation, and forecasting.

Real information can make the difference between a decision based on knowledge, and a guess. Real information can make the difference between a decision that contributes to improved marketing productivity, and no decision at all. In the latter case, an unproductive, perhaps deteriorating, marketing condition remains unexamined, and as is.

Information results from data that is processed and arranged in a certain way. Knowledge results from information that tells us something new, something we did not know before. Data can be numbers, letters, or symbols, but simply printing these numbers, letters, or symbols does not result in information.

When does data become information? Data becomes information, real or apparent, when expressed in a sentence:

☐ Orders booked YTD in sales territory 34 are $538,962.

☐ Travel and entertainment expense for 1980 was $397,118.

☐ There are twenty-two Model 1100's in Chicago inventory.

When does information become decision-oriented information for managers?

☐ When data is expressed as part of a sentence related to an expectation or plan. *YTD sales in territory 34 are $538,962, 24 percent below plan.* (We discuss this subject in Chapter 6.)

☐ When real information that contributes to knowledge is expressed. *There are six rep salespersons in territory 34. Four salespersons produced YTD sales of $538,962. The two sales areas with no YTD sales represent 37 percent of total prospects in territory 34.* This information could be produced by a Marketing Application Program (MAP) that listed YTD customers and prospects, by sales area, in territory 34. (We discuss this subject in Chapter 7.)

MANAGEMENT INFORMATION AND THE
TIME-PERISHABILITY OF DATA

Chapter 1 mentioned that the case for a formal, decision-oriented, information system in industrial marketing and sales is best made by the time-perishability of data for operating management purposes. We briefly expand on this idea now.

Business is made up of transactions. When the hundreds of thousands of business transactions with which a manufacturing company is involved each year are recorded, data is created. For management purposes, in general, data tends to be perishable over time. For operating management purposes, data tends to be *quickly* perishable over time.

As an example, sales managers in manufacturing companies where written quotations are an important pre-sale activity would find useful the following YTD comparisons of orders booked and quotations made, present and one year ago:

1. *By region.* In this example there are four sales regions.
2. *By rep territory.* There are forty rep territories.
3. *By rep salesperson.* There are 120 rep sales areas.
4. *By product.* There are thirty-eight products sold by this company.
5. *By customer type.* There are fifty different industrial classifications that make up the "customer base."
6. *By establishment size.* There are five "establishment size" classes of interest, and they vary within the fifty industrial classifications.

Obviously, the manual manipulation of the data used in constructing these reports would demand considerable effort. Perhaps less obvious, even if clerical expense associated with developing these reports manually could have been justified, opportunity for timely and appropriate management action was likely to have passed before comparative summaries were completed. The time-perishability of data for operating management purposes discouraged needed updating in pre-computer days.

Industrial marketing and sales managers have always required accurate, timely information updates in order to manage efficiently. Because necessary information updates have been beyond the capability of manual systems in most manufacturing companies, marketing and sales executives have had to learn to manage without some of the information that efficient marketing and sales management requires.

VALUE ANALYSIS IN INDUSTRIAL MARKETING AND SALES

Industrial marketing and sales managers require real information on which to base decisions that will contribute to increased operating efficiency and improved marketing productivity. Real information leads marketing and sales managers to where the gold is buried in industrial marketing and sales. Real information makes it possible to recover gold that has been hidden in waste and inefficiency. But real information, in addition to being new, must be true. It must also be accurate and precise.

Real information must be pertinent to the marketing productivity task. Real information can be new, true, accurate, precise, and irrelevant at the same time. Setting limits to what will be considered good and useful information is as important to information-gathering as collecting the information.

Information is obtained only by asking questions. The right kind of information is obtained only by asking the right kind of questions. Value analysis is an organized, methodical approach to asking the right kind of questions. The important real information required by marketing and sales managers can be developed by value analysis in industrial marketing and sales.

The subject of value analysis is well known. The techniques of value analysis are recognized for the contribution they make to corporate productivity. The fact that value analysis has been employed for years by large, well-managed companies is an endorsement that would appear to confirm its benefits.

Industrial marketing and sales managers are responsible for the efficient allocation of dollars of marketing and sales effort to products, sales territories, and customer classes. Traditional value analysis tends to be product-oriented. The suggestion made here is that the techniques of value analysis can be applied also to sales territories and customer classes.

Value analysis, when applied to a product, uses analytical method directed to the establishment of product value as well as cost. When we ask, "What does this product do?" we deal with the structure of the product. When we ask, "What *should* this product do?" we deal with the function of the product. Value analysis proceeds to methodically question:

1. What do the customers really want this product to do for them?
2. What do the customers want? How can they be given more of what they want?
3. What do the customers not want? How can they be given less of what they do not want?

4. What is the relative importance of the customers' wants? How can the product provide satisfaction of the customers' wants in proportion to their relative importance?
5. How can these things be accomplished at least cost?

Answers to these questions are apt to vary from product to product. They may also be expected to vary according to the characteristics and needs of sales territories and customer classes. Most of this book is a presentation of methods that can be employed to develop real information about individual products, sales territories, and customer classes.

Simple cost reduction concentrates on the decrease or elimination of expenditures. Value analysis, on the other hand, attempts to favorably influence profit margins by integrating product improvement (or the improvement of marketing and sales effort) with cost reduction.

What superhighways of information can be constructed over mountainous product, sales territory, and customer class data terrain? (See Chapter 1.) How can this information be used to help us get from A to B more efficiently, and in less time? What that is not presently known about products, sales territories, and customer classes would contribute to managerial knowledge, and enhance the decision-making capability of marketing and sales managers? These questions provide the framework for a formal, decision-oriented, information system in industrial marketing and sales management.

4

WHAT MARKETING AND SALES EXECUTIVES CAN LEARN FROM MRP

THE NEED FOR COMMON LANGUAGE

The Introduction to this book mentioned the urgent need for common language between marketing and sales managers and computer programmers. This book is a pioneer effort to encourage between these groups the dialogue essential to the development of marketing application programs that will improve productivity.

The systematic improvement of marketing productivity requires as well that marketing and sales managers share common language with accountants, and with production and inventory managers. Chapter 6 addresses accounting responsibilities that must be met before single-product marketing and sales costs can be isolated for marketing and sales management purposes. The chapter also offers an approach to resolving some of the accounting problems. This chapter is a discussion of what marketing and sales executives can learn from the production department's experience with material requirements planning (MRP).

INTRODUCTION TO MRP

Material requirements planning is a time-phased, order-scheduling technique that employs the massive raw data manipulation capability of the computer to rationalize production management and inventory control functions in manufacturing companies. Where manufacturers have successfully implemented MRP-based techniques, informal people systems have been replaced by formal procedure systems. Customer service has been upgraded, inventory investment reduced, and operating efficiency and plant productivity have been improved.

As discussed in Chapter 1, the computer's payoff in operating management applications results from the absence of satisfactory manual systems. The systems analysis required to rationalize operating management routines in order to accommodate the procedure-following demands of the computer can lead to a search for answers to operating questions no one bothered to ask before. Some of these new questions and answers form the basis for the written procedures that make formal, decision-oriented information systems possible in production departments. We refer to such procedures as MRP. We are interested in MRP to the extent that systems analysis, and subsequent development of procedures to rationalize production and inventory management functions, allow us to better understand problems we might expect to encounter in similar efforts to analyze and rationalize marketing and sales management activities.

Previously, we discussed the time-perishability of data for operating management purposes and the marginal value of information produced by computers. This helps explain on the one hand why operating departments in pre-computer days failed to develop formal procedure systems that worked and, on the other, why it is now important that they do so. To these points we would like to add a final comment regarding the nature of business organization.

Business organization is made up of individuals and groups, often with widely different organizational goals, and much of the time at least some of the goals are in conflict. The amount of conflict associated with the goals and objectives of various departments in business is variable. How much conflict can possibly exist among the goals and objectives of the payroll department, for example? Workers are paid according to known rates and for time periods that are well defined. Overtime is calculated according to a formula on which prior agreement has been reached. Taxes and other deductions are made in accordance with rules which are, at least, explainable. Vacation pay and sick pay are two more examples of calculations that tend to be straightforward and routine. Seen this way, it is not surprising that the payroll function within business organization yields easily to formally written manual procedures.

Compare the ease of developing formally written manual procedures in the payroll department, or any other support department where conflict among organizational goals is minimal, with the problems faced in this regard by operating departments where organizational goals and objectives are often in conflict. For example, the primary objectives of the production and inventory management departments in manufacturing companies are:

1. *Customer service.*   Because product delivery is basic to good customer service, the product ordered is either available for immediate delivery from inventory, or it can be manufactured and shipped to the customer within a competitively acceptable delivery time.
2. *Minimum inventory investment.*   The economics of inflation has forced corporate management to use money more efficiently by investing more intelligently. As a consequence, there is pressure in most manufacturing companies to accomplish company sales objectives with the least investment in inventory.
3   *Maximum plant operating efficiency.*   An increase in lot size decreases machine set-up time and ordering costs, while increasing the investment in inventory, and vice versa. A production schedule that allows the plant to run at a steady pace minimizes costs associated with hiring and training workers following layoffs, but there are tradeoffs here as well.

Because any one of the three objectives is only attainable at the expense of the other two, the primary objectives of production and inventory management are in conflict. The presence of such conflict in production departments did not encourage the development of formal procedure systems in pre-computer days.

There are other problems besides those resulting from conflicting objectives. In the real production world getting an order to the shipping dock on a promised date (while at the same time keeping inventory in line and operating the plant as efficiently as possible) is a more vital and important activity than trying to analyze why a particular part may have required expediting. It is not difficult to understand how these operating realities placed their own limit on efforts to rationalize production and inventory management routines.

Thinking in Different Mountain-Moving Categories about Production and Inventory Management

The operating problems of production and inventory management in manufacturing companies, and the MRP-based solutions brought to the problems, are too numerous and complicated to attempt to summarize here. But, by discussing a few examples of what resulted when production managers and systems analysts began thinking in the different categories made possible by the computer, we may be encouraged to begin to think in different categories about what we do in marketing and sales management as well.

Is MRP a solution to the production and inventory problems of every manufacturer? A company manufacturing a one-piece product, made-to-order for customers who are willing to wait a specified delivery time, does not need MRP. We might also place those firms manufacturing a one-piece product made-to-stock on a list of companies not inclined to view MRP as a top priority. Remaining, of course, are all the companies who manufacture assembled products, either made-to-order or made-to-stock—a description that applies to most contemporary manufacturing companies. It is accurate to say that a majority of these manufacturing companies are MRP candidates.

With regard, then, to manufacturing companies who produce assembled products, on either a made-to-order or made-to-stock basis, here are two examples of the results obtained by thinking in different categories about production and inventory management functions:

1. An assembled product is comprised of raw materials; raw materials are combined into fabricated components; fabricated components are joined together to become subassemblies; subassemblies eventually become assemblies; finally, assemblies are put together to form a finished product.

The classical order point system of inventory management assumes that demand for each inventory item is independent of all other items, and the item can therefore be independently ordered. Because a basic requirement of MRP is an up-to-date, complete, and accurate bill of material for each product, demand for many inventory items can be seen to be dependent. One item is only used in association with a second item. As a result, the important inventory management question changes from "How much and when to order?" to "When do we actually need to receive what we are ordering?"

In a production world where it is inefficiently commonplace to have on hand inventory items not presently needed, and not have on hand inventory items required to get a product out the door, this aspect of MRP represents a welcome new approach to the improvement of plant productivity.

2. The classical order point formula is:

$$OP = Dlt + SS$$

where: OP = order point
D = estimated demand
lt = lead time
SS = safety stock

MRP advocates, thinking in the different categories made possible by the computer, have reached the following conclusions regarding assumptions contained in this formula:

a. Although the order point is simple to calculate, one of its limitations is that it can only be correct for one theoretical moment. Because the production process itself creates inventory imbalances as a result of parts scrappage, short-order runs, and over-runs, order point calculations require constant inventory rebalancing if parts inventory is to remain accurate.

b. Lead time is the time required to replenish an item in inventory. Assumed in the order point formula to be a constant, it is in practice variable. Lead time variability also requires constant inventory rebalancing if parts inventory is to remain accurate.

c. Safety stock is calculated to protect against periods when demand *exceeds* forecast. There is no compensating adjustment for periods when demand is *less* than forecast. During such periods, safety stock can be thought of as an unnecessary investment in inventory. A more efficient system would adjust parts requirements for upside, as well as downside, forecast error.

From these few examples of thinking in different categories about production and inventory management, we can see the need for continuous inventory rebalancing if information updates for management purposes are to remain accurate. We have already mentioned that the updating requirement is beyond the capability of manual systems in most production departments. It is easy to understand why informal people systems developed to cope with the unceasing problems associated with getting products out the shipping room door on time. Other sources have referred to the presence of informal "order launching" and "expediting" systems in production departments without MRP.

Most companies are interested in satisfying customers with the best product delivery possible. Production and inventory management people have tended to schedule due dates on orders earlier than necessary to avoid accusation that they failed to order soon enough. Early due dates that are unrealistically scheduled lead to an operating condition where purchase orders and shop orders are typically late; and when all orders are late no order is late. In order to reestablish actual priorities, expediting is required. Expediting eventually determines which of the so-called late orders are really late orders but, unfortunately, it does so at the expense of high operating efficiency and plant productivity.

MRP utilizes the computer's massive raw data manipulation capability to isolate and explode material requirements, expressed in the assembly or subassembly sections of bills of material, into totals of each of the components required to produce a given quantity of the assembly or subassembly. Total material requirements are extrapolated from the master schedule and expressed in detail in specific time periods, usually weeks. The part of the MRP system that releases planned orders also keeps track of scheduling on materials already ordered, a sequence of updating routines not effectively accomplished manually before MRP.

Thinking in a few of the different categories the computer makes possible in production and inventory management allowed a distinction to be made between dependent and independent-demand inventory items that no one had bothered to make before. It also produced three questions no one had bothered to ask before challenging the assumptions of the classical order point formula. Aided by computer-based MRP scheduling techniques that provide a new way to keep complex, interrelated order priorities in manufacturing companies updated and realistic, it is not difficult to picture these few examples of rethinking the production function resulting in reduced inventory investment, increased operating efficiency, and improved plant productivity.

MRP is a powerful management tool in the right hands. By providing accurate, timely information in the planning, controlling, and updating of order priorities and plant capacities, MRP makes possible for the first time in production and inventory management a formal, decision-oriented, information system.

Thinking in Different Mountain-Moving Categories about Marketing and Sales Management

Perhaps the first step to be taken by marketing and sales executives interested in more effective utilization of the computer is to acknowledge that rethinking production and inventory management functions was not only possible, but fundamental to benefits gained. Such acknowledgment leads easily enough to contemplation of benefits to be similarly gained in marketing and sales management and of the possibilities that may exist for rethinking marketing and sales management functions. That such possibilities do exist will come as no surprise to those familiar with industrial marketing and sales management.

If production and inventory management without MRP is made up of informal people systems caught up in the frustration of conflicting departmental objectives, and in the *ad hoc* inefficiencies of "order launching" and "expediting" routines "to get the job done," a similar claim can be made with regard to marketing and sales management.

Informal, procedureless, seat-of-the-pants operating activities in industrial marketing and sales management are part of what has become a grand sales tradition, appearing to defy all effort to explain or rationalize. The uncertain, open-ended, conflicting nature of the goals and objectives of these departments, and the pre-computer lack of the ability to produce accurate, timely information updates for management purposes, combine to form marketing and sales organizations in many manufacturing companies where the irrational extent of, and dependence on, informal people systems "to get the job done" borders on the occult. In light of these circumstances, if something less than a profound rationalization of industrial marketing and sales management routines is all that can be expected from these pioneer efforts to think in different categories made possible by the computer, significant increase in operating efficiency and improved marketing productivity are certain to be gained.

Does every manufacturing company selling to an industrial market need to concern itself with the rationalizing requirements of a formal, decision-oriented, information system in marketing and sales management? Companies that manufacture products for sale to one customer are unlikely to realize great benefit from efforts to rationalize marketing and sales management activities. Companies that sell to a handful of customers they know well, and perhaps supply on the basis of successfully negotiated annual purchase contracts, and companies operating in regional markets where the customer base is limited, are unlikely to consider a formal, decision-oriented, information system in marketing and sales management a top priority.

Remaining, however, are all the companies that stand to gain the most from such an information system. These are the small-to-medium size manufacturing companies selling to industrial markets:

☐ where scope is national and international

☐ where a central characteristic is fast growth and diversity of product use in a multiplicity of market segments that, from a marketing point of view, are not well defined

☐ where there are several distribution channels, and at least one is probably understaffed from the point of view of optimal sales coverage, or

☐ where a single distribution channel is so densely populated by geographically spread and functionally diverse distributor, rep, and customer class groupings that management control of marketing and sales effort is adversely affected

☐ where technology is fast developing and emergent, making accurate forecasts of product life cycles impossible

☐ where competition is keen, market share a guess, and uncertainty about the future is great

☐ where total marketing and sales costs are higher than desired, and

☐ where custodial accounting systems in companies selling multiproduct lines do not make single-product marketing and sales costs known, disallowing control of revenue-cost relationships at the management level required to methodically increase operating efficiency and improve marketing productivity.

The limits time and human nature place on individual experience and knowledge prohibit a rethinking of marketing and sales management functions applicable to all companies. What we can wish to provide here are comments that may be found useful, and examples of what has already been done. Hopefully, marketing and sales managers, together with systems analysts and computer programmers, will thus be inspired to begin the rethinking process for themselves.

Order-Filling vs. Order-Getting Activities

Rethinking industrial marketing and sales management functions so that an early distinction is made between "order-filling" and "order-getting" activities substantially reduces the rationalizing task. We can think about order-filling activities as mostly intra-organizational. In the interests of order-processing efficiency and delivery promises to be kept, an order-by-order updating of intentions and priorities by sales and production departments is required. The work to be done in order to rationalize marketing and sales management functions, then, is reduced to the extent that order-filling activities in the sales department are influenced by MRP-based scheduling techniques that support order-filling activities in the production department. As might be guessed, such influence is large.

The primary task in marketing and sales management is to think about order-getting activities in different categories made possible by the computer so that some of these activities may be rationalized by a formal, decision-oriented, information system. Note here that order-getting activities are, for the most part, activities associated with various combinations of the marketing mix.

It has been stated that the aim of this book is to get industrial marketing and sales executives involved in getting more effective computing done in their departments. Toward this end we have included, in Chapter 8, examples of Marketing Application Programs, or MAPs, that have been employed for specific order-getting purposes. This section concludes with a discussion of three MAPs, emphasizing the rethinking of marketing and sales management activities that provided the framework for their design and development:

1. MAP QF-1A of Chapter 8 is made possible by the establishment of a computer "quotation file" in manufacturing com-

panies where pre-sale quotation activity is an order-getting requirement. In keeping with the format of this book, MAP QF-1A is explained by commentary on its facing page. It is introduced here as an example of one result of thinking in different categories about the company master schedule.

The company master schedule can be thought of as the place where order-filling activities in the sales department and order-filling activities in the production department merge. It has been claimed that any uncertainty associated with MRP-based scheduling techniques resides in the master schedule.

Whether the company manufactures to finished goods inventory, or according to a backlog of orders booked, it is unlikely that items scheduled for manufacture represent firm orders all the time. In master scheduling items for manufacture where firm orders do not exist, MAP QF-1A provides information to further assure the integrity of the master schedule by the application of subjective probability to order-getting expectations contained in anticipated closing quotations in the quotation file.

2.   MAP CF-1A of Chapter 8 is one result of thinking in different categories about sales "leads." It is not unfair to say that conventional wisdom among marketing and sales managers holds that the sales lead is an indispensable ticket to success in industrial market places. It is not unfair to say, either, that the total amount of time and money spent generating and following-up sales leads is wastefully large; and that most sales lead systems are inefficiently administered.

Most sales leads are developed as the result of responses to advertising and sales promotion. They tend to be random and of mixed quality. MAP CF-1A results from a formal, proceduralized approach to gathering unique, highly qualified, sales lead information from a typically overlooked source—the customer list.

Discussed in detail in Chapter 7, this method, which is applicable to companies with existing customer lists, exposes sales leads obtained from advertising and sales promotion for what they are: necessary and desirable, but expensive and distinctly second best.

If marketing and sales executives are exclusively supervising the chasing of random sales leads, while ignoring the information that may reside in customer lists, they have not been thinking long enough in different categories the computer makes possible.

3.   MAP SF-1A of Chapter 8 results from thinking in different categories about market penetration. This MAP will serve to empha-

size that marketing and sales executives in manufacturing companies have as fertile ground for rethinking marketing and sales management functions as their counterparts in production and inventory management.

With regard to the measurement of market penetration, unless a company is confident that the rate of market growth and some external factor, as GNP, are coincident, it is not possible to deal objectively with this subject. Also, the measurement of market penetration for management purposes does not mean much unless market segments are also identified and measured. These numbers would derive from some expression of market saturation by segment, but how? It is all rather frustrating.

The consequence of the inability to exact objective measurement of market penetration leads to more wishful "talking around" the subject than factual talk. Last year's market penetration "success" may have resulted from a windfall of large, one-time, orders; and only fair or poor results in other order value classes. This year's "failure" to penetrate markets may actually reflect excellent penetration in certain order value classes and market segments, with much future promise; and no large, one-time, orders to pursue.

MAP SF-1A is an analysis that compares relative market penetration, by order value class, in two operating periods. It is only one of several ways in which market penetration may be measured, but there is revealed by this MAP a great deal of the kind of decision-making information the computer can be programmed to provide. The three MAPs discussed here, and eleven more MAPs involving order-getting activities in industrial marketing and sales management, are each presented with a detailed commentary in Chapter 8.

PART THREE

THE LOWDOWN ON HIGH MARKETING PRODUCTIVITY

5

MARKETING
PRODUCTIVITY ANALYSIS

SOME MEASURES OF PRODUCTIVITY

Productivity is the interrelationship between input and output. Chapter 3 mentioned that the concept of productivity, as compared to efficiency, is dynamic in the sense that it refers to a generative source of *continuing* activity. Marketing productivity depends upon the generation of information to enhance decision-making in marketing and sales management on a *continuing* basis.

Whether the measurement is one of efficiency or productivity, students of elementary physics know that if output increases faster than input, there is gain; and if output decreases in relation to input, there is loss. It is all so simple that productivity is a subject everyone thinks he or she understands. However, understanding the concept of productivity in general, and making informed decisions to improve the productivity of a particular marketing and sales organization, are two different subjects. This book is about using the computer to improve marketing productivity in manufacturing companies selling to industrial markets, so we need now to discuss some common methods used to measure productivity, and explain why they are not useful to marketing and sales managers.

There are a number of ways corporate productivity can be measured that are so broad and general that the concept of productivity is obscured. Take sales output per labor-hour as an example. Sales, adjusted to constant dollars to compensate for price changes, are divided by total labor-hours in an operating period so that comparisons of different operating periods can be made.

TABLE 5.1
A Typical Measurement of Productivity—ABC Company

	Operating Periods		
	1	2	3
Sales in constant dollars	$1,000,000	$1,200,000	$1,300,000
Labor-hours	40,000	48,000	50,000
Sales output/labor-hour	$25	$25	$26
Percent productivity change	—	—	+ 4

Although Table 5.1 summarizes changes in productivity for the ABC Company, specific areas of productivity change are not revealed. While the productivity increase in Operating Period 3 is impressive, nothing explains why it occurred. Unless ABC is a single product manufacturer, or sells a homogeneous product line in a relatively constant mix, the fact that plant and marketing productivity are not separately analyzed fails to provide essential information to the operating managers responsible for productivity.

There are variations on the output per labor-hour, or sales per employee, approach that provide more precise information. For example, where units of output are used in place of sales dollars, inaccuracies associated with adjusting sales to constant dollars can be eliminated. There are also methods of weighting units so that product mix differences can be expressed using standard labor-hours required to produce items sold. But marketing and sales executives responsible for the sale of heterogeneous product lines, where product mix may vary, are provided no useful management information by these summaries.

MARKETING PRODUCTIVITY DEFINED FOR MANAGERS

Having dismissed general productivity measures as useless to operating managers, we would like to present a working definition of marketing productivity helpful to managers in industrial marketing and sales. The definition that follows was first encountered in Charles H. Sevin's *Marketing Productivity Analysis.* * Many of the ideas about marketing productivity expressed here were first encountered in Sevin's book.

---

*From *Marketing Productivity Analysis* by Charles H. Sevin. Copyright © 1965. Used with the permission of McGraw-Hill Book Company.

Marketing productivity is defined as the sales or net profit output per *unit* of marketing effort, and is expressed as a ratio—of sales or net profit to marketing and sales costs—for *individual products, sales territories,* and *customer classes.*

The information required to satisfy such detailed analysis has, in the past, exceeded the capability of most custodial accounting systems in manufacturing companies. As a consequence, the productivity aspect of industrial marketing and sales management has been ignored. Fortunately, the computer's massive raw data manipulation capability can be used to generate the detailed information updates needed to methodically improve marketing productivity in manufacturing companies selling to industrial markets.

When the contribution to net profit is made known by individual product, sales territory, or customer class, marketing productivity may be improved five ways:

1. If an increase in sales or net profit is proportionately greater than a corresponding increase in marketing and sales costs (see (1), Figure 5.1)
2. If an increase in sales or net profit is achieved with the same marketing and sales costs (see (2), Figure 5.1)
3. If an increase in sales or net profit is achieved with decreased marketing and sales costs (see (3), Figure 5.1)
4. If the same sales or net profit is achieved with decreased marketing and sales costs (see (4), Figure 5.1)
5. If a decrease in sales or net profit is proportionately less than a corresponding decrease in marketing and sales costs (see (5), Figure 5.1).

Table 5.2 compares present net profit to net profit results derived from each of the approaches to the improvement of marketing productivity we have defined. Table 5.2 can be used in two ways:

1. To demonstrate the value to managers of the marketing productivity concept as compared to the simplistic "increase sales, increase profit" approach.
2. To demonstrate the leverage of marketing and sales costs phenomena on net profit. The large changes in net profit occasioned by relatively small changes in sales, and below-the-line, direct, incremental marketing and sales expense, should be of interest to managers.

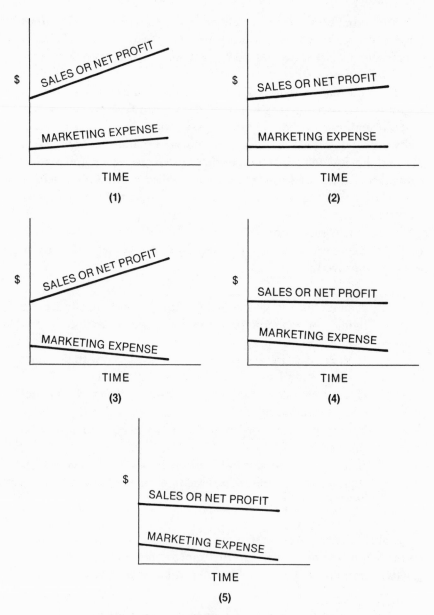

FIGURE 5.1
Five Ways Marketing Productivity May Be Improved

TABLE 5.2
Five Marketing Productivity Methods: Pro-Forma Income Statements—ABC Company (thousands)

	Present	1	2	3	4	5
Sales (100%)	1,000	+10% 1,100	1,100	1,100	1,000	−4.5% 955
Cost of Goods Sold (40%)	400	440	440	440	400	382
Gross margin (60%)	600	660	660	660	600	573
Operating expense: Direct, incremental marketing & sales expense	300(30%)	+5% 315(28.6%)	300(27.3%)	−5% 285(25.9%)	285(28.5%)	−8.3% 275(28.8%)
Programmed & standby costs	240(24%)	240(21.8%)	240(21.8%)	240(21.8%)	240(24%)	240(25.1%)
Net profit	60(6%)	+75% 105(9.6%)	+100% 120(10.9%)	+125% 135(12.3%)	+25% 75(7.5%)	−3.3% 58(6.1%)

In Column 1, sales are up by 10 percent, marketing and sales expense is up by 5 percent, and net profit is up by *75* percent. In Column 2, sales are up by 10 percent, marketing and sales expense unchanged, and net profit is up by *100* percent. In Column 3, sales are up by 10 percent, marketing and sales expense is down by 5 percent, and net profit has increased *125* percent. In Column 4, sales are unchanged, marketing and sales expense is down 5 percent, and net profit is up *25* percent. In Column 5, sales are down by about 4 percent, marketing and sales expense has decreased a little over 8 percent, and net profit is down around 3 percent.

MARKETING MIX INEFFICIENCIES

No company realizes equal net profit from the sale of every product it markets. Some products contribute to net profit at higher rates than other products. It may even be true that some products contribute to net profit at negative rates. Each product shares a segment, or segments, of the market with competitive products. Each product in the product "mix" of the typical multiproduct manufacturing company tends to require various combinations of marketing and sales expenditures making up the company's marketing mix. The marketing mix of expenditures is the investment made by management to assure the sale of products the company manufactures.

Because single-product marketing and sales costs are not reported by custodial accounting systems in an accurate, timely manner, the following marketing mix misallocations are common in industrial marketing and sales departments:

1. *Single-product marketing and sales expenditures are too large.* If marketing and sales expenditures for any one product were arbitrarily increased from one operating period to the next, resulting sales volume would eventually begin to increase at a decreasing rate, and the incremental investment in marketing effort would be subject to diminishing returns. As there is a limit to the size of markets at any one time and, in competitive market places, a limit to market share at any one time, sooner or later the contribution to net profit made by this product would decrease and become negative. Despite such evidence, particularly when decisions must be made without detailed information updates, the tendency is

to place bets on past winners. Where the sale of products is subject to diminishing returns, reallocating marketing expenditures to products where rates of diminishing returns are less, or where there are increasing returns, would increase operating efficiency and improve marketing productivity.

2. *Single-product marketing and sales expenditures are too small.* This is a corollary to number 1. Marketing productivity gains would follow, adding to the dollars of marketing effort invested in products that bring increasing returns, or where the rate of diminishing returns is less than other products.

3. *Single-product marketing and sales expenditures are inefficiently combined.* Whether too much or too little is invested in product advertising, as compared to other forms of sales promotion, personal selling, or quantity pricing, other combinations of the components of the marketing mix would improve marketing productivity.

4. *The marketing mix is misallocated among products, sales territories, and customer classes.* If the level of marketing expenditures remained the same, reallocating the marketing mix among products, sales territories, and customer classes would increase sales and profit, and improve marketing productivity.

THE 80/20 RULE

In production and inventory management, ABC classifications rank inventory items by annual usage in dollars. A relatively few inventory items typically represent most of the inventory dollars. With the help of ABC classifications, managers can concentrate inventory control efforts on items that make up the largest part of inventory investment.

In industrial marketing and sales management the ABC classification becomes the 80/20 rule. The 80/20 rule and marketing productivity are intimately related. According to definition, industrial marketing productivity is expressed as the ratio of sales or net profit (output) to marketing and sales costs (input) for *individual products, sales territories,* and *customer classes.* The 80/20 rule suggests that some of these input-output relationships are disproportionate; in other words, Pareto, or "distribution by value," phenomena exist in the marketing universe.

Most industrial marketing and sales managers would probably affirm that *about* 20 percent of the sales force produces *about* 80 percent of the sales volume. But the "distribution by value" subject in marketing and sales management is rarely further entertained. The 80/20 rule requires a strict and formal observance by these managers if marketing productivity is to be methodically improved.

Here are some examples of unequal product, sales territory, and customer class distributions that require identification and updating for marketing and sales management purposes. This is a large task in most manufacturing companies, now eased by the massive raw data manipulation capability of the computer:

1.   Relatively few products make up most of sales, and relatively few products make up most of net profit. When single-product marketing and sales costs are made known, the product contribution to sales and the product contribution to net profit can be compared.

In Table 5.3, the top five products are responsible for 79 percent of sales, and about 86 percent of net profit. But the rates at which these products contribute to net profit, *after* marketing and sales costs, are greatly variable. For example, two products (A and E) make up nearly 60 percent of net profit. Seven products made negative contributions to net profit. Some of these were recent introductions to the market and early loss was anticipated. But the information presented in Table 5.3 clearly shows product concentrations in terms of sales and net profit, and allows managers to cut losses early by eliminating unsuccessful products or, by comparing relative rates of net profit contribution by product, reallocate dollars of marketing effort to optimize input-output relationships and improve marketing productivity.

2.   The concentration of industrial markets is well known. Relatively few sales territories make up most of sales and net profit. While this disproportion may reflect concentrations of demand for a company's products, it is also true that territories with the most sales and territories with the most prospects need not be the same territories.

The concentration of distributor and rep firms parallels the concentration of industrial markets. But the problems a manufacturer may have selecting the best representation for its products in sales territories can be complicated by the concentration of product lines offered by distributors and reps. Selling priorities, and the buyer pro-

TABLE 5.3
Sales and Net Profit Contributions Made by Products

Product	% Net Sales	% Net Profit
All Products	100.0	100.0
A	18.3	32.4
B	17.5	8.6
C	17.2	10.1
D	15.1	7.5
E	10.9	27.2
F	3.8	7.5
G	3.1	8.4
H	2.4	− 3.3
I	2.0	4.0
J	1.6	3.4
K	1.2	2.5
L	1.1	1.7
M	1.0	− 2.5
N	1.0	2.5
O	0.9	1.5
P	0.9	− 1.6
Q	0.8	− 2.5
R	0.5	− 2.5
S	0.5	− 1.6
T	0.2	− 3.3

file attracted by available product lines, may make a particular distributor or rep firm the correct choice for every manufacturer represented except one.

3. Relatively few customer classes make up most of sales, and relatively few customer classes make up most of net profit. The development of information regarding concentrations of profitable, less profitable, and unprofitable customer classes allows managers to reallocate dollars of marketing effort and improve marketing productivity.

Presented here are only a few of many examples of "distribution by value" phenomena in the marketing universe. The concentrations described by the 80/20 rule challenge the reason and imagination of marketing and sales managers to allocate dollars of marketing effort to products, sales territories, and customer classes so that input-output relationships are optimized and high marketing productivity achieved.

The marketing and sales world is large, diversified, and often complicated. Computer-based analysis revealing concentrations of sales and net profit among relatively few products, sales territories, and customer classes also reveals unprofitable areas. What is to be done with the unprofitable, or low profit, products, sales territories, and customer classes?

Alternatives range from simple elimination or improvement, to leaving them (for what may be excellent reasons) as they are. Because eliminating all inefficiency is not possible, and may not be desirable, prudent managers concentrate efforts on those areas under their control that are most likely to influence the results they are attempting to achieve. Managers who will succeed best in the improvement of marketing productivity are those individuals who seek to advance their projects one step at a time. Most of the inefficiency surrounding industrial marketing and sales management has developed over time. People are involved. Their beliefs, habits, and organizational inertia need consideration and appraisal; perhaps a long-term educational program is a basic requirement. Whatever the case, no number of algebraic formulations and analytical techniques in marketing and sales management will convert inefficiency to efficiency once and for all. The wise marketing or sales managers know this.

In the book referred to earlier in this chapter, Sevin devotes a number of chapters to what he calls "marketing experiments." These are marketing and sales situations where improvements in marketing productivity depend on the development of information to be derived from controlled experimentation and simulation. In my industrial marketing and sales management experience, there has been little time, money, or inclination for such experimenting. As the attempt to methodically improve marketing productivity is begun, the major opportunities do not usually require experimentally developed information before an early and appropriate management action may be taken. Because we are resolved to proceed a step at a time, we are wise to take the most obvious steps first.

6

MANAGING MARKETING COSTS AND PROFITABILITY

As we begin a chapter in which some of the deficiencies of custodial accounting information for marketing and sales management purposes are discussed, it is appropriate to note that accountants typically understand no more about marketing and sales management functions than do computer people. Yet, marketing and sales managers require the cooperation of accounting managers and computer programmers if formal, decision-oriented, information systems are to be developed in marketing and sales management.

Although we are reminded that long journeys begin with a single step, we are not always told the first step may be the most difficult to take. The first step to be taken by marketing and sales managers who are interested in obtaining managerial accounting information, is to educate themselves regarding the objectives of custodial accounting systems. They must then convince accounting managers that computerized restructuring of the Chart of Accounts is necessary if managerial accounting information is to be generated. Marketing and sales managers are at some disadvantage in this undertaking. They are not accountants. It is never easy to engage in conversation where fluency in language is one-sided; let alone be persuasive enough to make others willing to accomplish what, without them, would remain unaccomplished.

The subject of custodial accounting is large, but we do what we can in one chapter to provide insights that ease the management information task for marketing and sales managers, as well as accounting managers.

WHAT IS WRONG WITH CUSTODIAL ACCOUNTING?

The performance of marketing and sales management should be measured against that which is controlled; namely, price, volume, mix, and budgetary variances. Custodial accounting, preoccupied with period costs and full absorption costing, and in general not structured to accurately report price, volume, and mix variances, can so distort marketing and sales results as to greatly frustrate managers involved. Because we contend here that the nature of custodial accounting systems puts informed decision-making by marketing and sales managers at a disadvantage, it is appropriate that we discuss custodial accounting principles in somewhat greater detail.

Custodial accounting is a caretaking accounting function oriented to the external interests of a business. In this sense, the custodial accounting system "takes care" to accurately report the condition of a business to stockholders, interested lenders, security exchanges, banks, and government. Custodial accounting reports are historical and they summarize what has happened over the course of an operating period, often in great detail. Despite the time-honored status and importance of custodial accounting, however, dissecting the company's financial past provides token information, at best, to operating managers whose responsibility and craft is to make decisions to assure the company's future.

There was a time when custodial accounting was adequate for operating management purposes. At the turn of this century, the products of most manufacturing firms were not so widely differentiated as they are today. Where the products of one firm are so much like the products of other firms that product differentiation is nonexistent, all firms are, at management levels, mainly involved with planning the rate of the flow of goods. They are "quantity adapters." The marketing function in such firms is not very different from the production function.

The following custodial accounting concepts form the basis for external reports. One hundred years ago, they did not seriously handicap the informational needs of marketing and sales managers:

1. *The period cost.* This is a concept that matches revenues with the costs necessary to produce the revenues in an operating period. Helpful in assuring consistency in accounting methods from one time period to another and from one business to another, period costing arbitrarily overlooks the possibility that costs incurred in one time period may produce revenues in subsequent time periods.

Unlike earlier days of essentially nondifferentiated products, contemporary manufacturing companies actively seek the favor of customers in their marketplaces by product differentiation. The marketing function, once not easily distinguished from the production function, is today an area of managerial interest that may extend from a point long before the actual production process begins to a time and place far beyond the sale of the product. Because there may be a number of differentiated products available for sale, each requiring its own mix of marketing effort, requirements for accurate, timely marketing and sales management information have changed.

Custodial accounting systems in most manufacturing companies, however, remain the same. The need to report the financial condition of marketing ventures—ventures involving differentiated products where revenue-cost relationships may not be accurately matched by operating period—is sacrificed to the need to report the financial condition of the enterprise.

2. *Full absorption costing.* This is a concept that assigns all direct and indirect manufacturing costs to products, carrying these costs through inventory into cost of sales. While full absorption costing serves the needs of the custodial accounting system, depending on how the basis for absorption is calculated it can also distort the operating picture marketing and sales managers are trying to see.

If, as earlier stated, total marketing and sales costs in many manufacturing companies are the largest of all costs as a percentage of the sales dollar, the managerial control of these costs demands they be identified by individual product in a differentiated, multiproduct line. But dollars of marketing effort expended on an individual product, sales territory, or customer class are not accurately reported by custodial accounting systems.

It is true as well that some marketing costs are not reported as marketing costs at all. They may simply be classified in other categories, and buried in manufacturing costs or general and administrative expenses. This is one way marketing costs are distorted by a custodial accounting system. Here are two other examples of costs that may be distorted by arbitrary allocations:

1. Allocation of marketing costs to individual products, sales territories, and customer classes on the basis of sales volume
2. Allocation of general and administrative costs to business segments on the basis of sales volume.

There is nothing inherently wrong with natural-expense account classifications employed in custodial accounting. Similarly, there is nothing inherently wrong with custodial accounting systems that neatly, if arbitrarily, match revenue and expense in an operating period so that results can be reported to the outside world. However, in the modern industrial marketing world, there is something wrong with trying to make operating management decisions on the basis of custodial accounting information. This is particularly the case when the massive raw data manipulation capability of the computer is available for generating information about products, sales territories, and customer classes which enhances the decision-making capabilities of industrial marketing and sales managers. We need to learn how to instruct the computer so that important, decision-oriented, managerial accounting information is provided.

NATURAL EXPENSE VS. FUNCTIONAL EXPENSE CLASSIFICATIONS

It was mentioned earlier that the subject of custodial accounting is large, but that we would do what we could in a single chapter to ease the burden of dialogue that must take place between marketing and sales managers and accountants if essential managerial accounting information is to be produced. The subject of natural-expense, as opposed to functional-expense, classifications is a good place to start.

The custodial accounting system is historically biased toward financial reportage to outside groups. Not surprisingly, accountants tend to inherit that bias. Consequently, they may appear more willing to teach custodial accounting principles to managers than undertake the hard work associated with development of the managerial accounting information that marketing and sales managers really need.

It is important that accounting managers understand from the outset that functional-expense classifications are intended to managerially augment, not replace, natural-expense classifications; and that the computer's space, total recall capability, and speed (see Chapter 2) make possible a massive raw data manipulation capability that permits these two methods of reporting costs to exist separately, side-by-side.

It is a matter of keeping primary-expense accounts in sufficient detail. Many companies continue to work with Charts of Accounts that were appropriate in pre-computer days, *after* they have acquired a computer. These Charts of Accounts are inadequate for computer-based information systems. A relatively simple account coding structure is needed that can be expanded from a few digits to many digits to accommodate the requirements of these information systems. There are three areas of marketing and sales costs reported by custodial accounting systems that, for marketing and sales management purposes, require reclassification:

1. The marketing and sales costs buried in general and administrative expense need to be reidentified as marketing and sales costs, and appropriately classified.

2. Direct and separable marketing and sales costs need to be classified in sufficient detail in primary-expense accounts so that they may be accurately assigned to individual products, sales territories, and customer classes.

3. Indirect and nonseparable marketing and sales costs need to be reclassified functionally, with each functional-expense group allocated to products, sales territories, and customer classes on the basis of "cost control" factors. Which activities tend to increase, or decrease, a cost? What is the cause of a cost?

Tables 6.1 and 6.2 represent functional-expense classifications in order-getting and order-filling activities in marketing and sales. By bringing together all costs associated with each order-getting and order-filling activity, marketing and sales expenditures can be more accurately determined by individual product, sales territory, and customer class than when arbitrarily allocated on the basis of a factor such as sales volume.

Marketing and sales managers can better manage marketing costs and profitability when functional-expense classifications are allocated to individual products, sales territories, and customer classes on the basis of measurable factors that have causal relationships to totals. It must be remembered that part of the appeal of natural-expense classifications includes the ease of being arbitrary. It is not easy to classify marketing and sales costs functionally.

What happens, for example, when a natural-expense item represents the performance of several functions? What happens when marketing and sales costs are grouped by function, and the same cost is direct measured one way, and indirect measured another way?

TABLE 6.1
Order-Getting Costs by Function

*Costs Common to Some Functional Categories:**
Salaries and wages
Training
Insurance
Taxes
Pensions
Rent
Supplies
Utilities
Depreciation
Maintenance

Direct Selling
Common costs*
Commissions
Travel and entertainment
Returned goods expense

Advertising and Sales Promotion
Common costs*
Publication space
Product promotion
Advertising agency fees
Direct-mail expense
Conventions and shows
Catalogs and price lists
Coop. advertising

Market Research
Common costs*
Surveys
Industry trade data
Travel and entertainment

Technical Product Service
Common costs*
Laboratory materials
Factory pilot and experimental costs
Research requests
Engineering requests
Product packages and design
Travel and entertainment

Warranty Costs
Warranty claims
Advertising material—warranty claims

Credit Extension
Common costs*
Credit rating services
Legal fees—collection efforts
Bad debt losses
Financial cost of carrying accounts receivable

Sales Discounts and Allowances
Cash discount on sales
Quantity discounts
Sales allowances

TABLE 6.2
Order-Filling Costs by Function

Costs Common to Some
Functional Categories: *

Salaries and wages	*Rent*
Training	*Supplies*
Insurance	*Utilities*
Taxes	*Depreciation*
Pensions	*Maintenance*

Warehousing and Handling
Common costs*
Unsalable merchandise—warehouse respon-
sibility

Inventory Levels
Obsolescence markdowns
Financial cost of carrying inventory

Order Processing
Common costs*
Returned goods processing

Billing and Recording of Accounts Receivable
Common costs*
Sales invoice forms

Obviously, these determinations are part of the work accountants perform. It is not marketing and sales managers who will decide these things. But where it is necessary to spread natural-expense items among several functional-expense classifications, are not work-measurement studies, space occupied, number of invoice lines, or management estimates better than no effort at all to functionally classify marketing and sales costs?

An important difference between custodial accounting and managerial accounting relates to the changing identification and behavior of costs as the object of measurement (product, sales territory, customer class) changes. It must, however, be remembered that the ability to identify and sort the cost, as either direct or indirect, results from detailed cost coding in the Chart of Accounts and the computer's massive raw data manipulation capability.

GROSS PROFIT VS. PROFIT CONTRIBUTION

As stated in the Introduction to this book, it is assumed the reader is familiar with the fundamentals of accounting. But, in order to appreciate the potentially disadvantageous influence of custodial accounting information on marketing and sales management decisions, marketing and sales managers need to understand the difference between gross profit and profit contribution. So we briefly summarize what is meant by these terms here.

Gross profit is a custodial accounting term, and is the difference between sales and cost of goods sold. In accordance with custodial accounting principles, the cost of goods sold is fully absorbed. In other words, all manufacturing costs that can conceivably be matched with sales or revenue are included. All nonmatchable costs incurred during an operating period appear in the profit and loss statement as a selling expense, or as a general and administrative expense.

Profit contribution is a marginal income concept, and is the difference between sales and all variable costs, regardless of whether the variable cost is incurred in manufacturing, sales, or administration. Profit contribution is an analysis of cost that allows marketing and sales managers to determine the contribution made by an individual product (or product line) to corporate overhead and profit. Because there is profit contribution that can be identified and controlled, for each unit sold each time a unit is sold, profit contribution is decision-oriented, managerial accounting information.

Clearly, the value of gross margin statements lies in standards adhered to by custodial accounting systems for purposes of reporting the financial condition of the enterprise. All costs incurred during an operating period must be matched against all revenues realized during the same period. Costs not directly assignable, as corporate overhead, are allocated to products in the manner we have discussed.

Custodial accounting is neat, tidy, and financially conservative in keeping with accounting principles. But marketing and sales managers who are responsible for making the correct decisions about products, sales territories, and customer classes, on the basis of gross margin information, may be working with distorted cost representations. Profit contribution statements serve these managers better. A favorite rhetorical ploy of those steeped in custodial accounting tradition is: How does one know if there will be enough profit contribution by products to provide for corporate overhead and profit? The answer to this is that desired total profit contribution is a function of planning, not overhead absorption. In managerial accounting, total profit contribution of all products equals corporate overhead plus profit. Planning should determine the combination of price, volume, and product mix required in order to yield the total profit contribution desired.

PLANNING MARKETING COSTS AND PROFITABILITY

There are five cost categories of interest to marketing and sales executives. Three of these categories can be planned and controlled by these managers directly. One cost category, beyond the control of marketing and sales managers, introduces the idea of standard manufacturing costs as a planning tool. All cost categories are represented in Table 6.3, an outline of a profit contribution statement by product or product line.

1. *Sales deductions and allowances.* These costs are the difference between gross sales and net sales, and include cash discounts, commissions, trade allowances, and freight out. These are variable costs, incurred in direct relationship to the number of sales made, and they can be planned and controlled by marketing and sales managers.

TABLE 6.3
Statement of Earnings by Product or Product Line: Year Ending 19___, ABC Company

			Product or Product Line			
	Company Total	Per Unit	"A" Total	Per Unit	"B" Total	Per Unit
Gross sales	$	$	$	$	$	$
Variable costs						
Cash discounts						
Commissions						
Trade allowances						
Freight out						
Net sales						
Direct materials						
Direct labor						
Variable overhead						
Total variable costs	$	$	$	$	$	$
Profit contribution	$ %		$ %		$ %	

Specific product expenses—programmed			
Selling			
Sales contest			
Advertising mgr.			
Merchandising mgr.			
Direct mail			
Displays			
Shows			
Trade publications			
Samples			
Travel and entertainment			
Cost of returns	$		
Total		$	
Administrative			
Professional fees			
Travel			
Trade associations			
Provision for doubtful accounts	$		
Total		$	
Total specific product expense		$	
Product earnings		$	
General expenses—standby			
Selling	$		
Administrative	$		
Manufacturing	$		
Earnings before taxes	$		

2. *Manufacturing costs.*   These direct material and direct labor costs are not controlled by marketing and sales managers, but are of interest because of their impact on profit contribution. As future sales and profit activity levels are planned by marketing and sales managers, they must insist that a standard manufacturing cost is established for each product, with appropriate variances shown as labor and material costs change during a planning cycle. In companies dependent on custodial accounting systems for management information, it is not unusual for marketing and sales managers to be held accountable for the adverse effect on the sales and profit plan of price increases, for example, attributable to changes in manufacturing cost.

3. *Variable overhead.*   These are manufacturing, sales, and administrative costs that are normally recurring, but are not specifically assignable to a unit of production. They vary directly, in some manner, with volume.

   These three cost categories represent planned, direct, and incremental costs. By subtracting the total of these variable costs, by product, from the product's gross sales price, the product profit contribution to fixed, nonincremental, programmed, and standby costs and pre-tax earnings can be determined.

4. *Programmed costs.*   These fixed costs are incurred as the result of management decision. Although they can be increased or decreased by management decision, a company is usually committed to these costs for a planning period. Advertising, travel and entertainment, sales contests, and trade shows are examples.

5. *Standby costs.*   These are fixed costs that would be incurred at zero sales volume, as long as the company wished to continue in business. Salaries of officers and key management personnel, rent, property taxes, and depreciation are examples.

It has been suggested in past chapters that the contribution to corporate overhead and profit by individual products, after marketing and sales costs, is either not accurately reported or not reported at all by custodial accounting systems. Having access to accurate, product contribution information, as it might appear in Table 6.3, makes it possible for marketing and sales managers to (1) plan and control specific product marketing and sales expense, (2) identify and isolate problem areas, and (3) more efficiently allocate the dollars of marketing effort, represented by the marketing mix, among products, sales territories, and customer classes. It is in this manner that marketing productivity is methodically improved.

EXCEPTION REPORTING

The determination of standard manufacturing cost for individual products isolates the variables that are under the control of marketing and sales managers. These variables, as set forth in the plan, are price, volume, product mix, and budgeted cost. Managerial accounting information describes the effect on planned profit of deviations from plan analyzed in terms of these variables:

1. *Price variance.* The effect on planned profit of deviations from planned selling prices after allowances for normal discounts.
2. *Volume variance.* The effect on planned profit of deviations from planned sales volume.
3. *Product mix variance.* The effect on planned profit of deviations from planned sales mix.
4. *Budgeted cost variance.* The effect on planned profit of deviations from planned expense levels.

As mentioned in Chapter 3, data is numbers arranged according to a pattern, and information is data arranged in sentences. Management information is sentences relating information to some expectation or plan. The massive raw data manipulation capability of the computer can be used to sort managerial accounting information so that only important deviations from plan are reported to managers. As long as a plan exists, and tolerable deviations from plan established, exception reporting is possible. This important advantage of sales and profit planning can be a significant time-saving tool for companies interested in improving marketing productivity.

We began this chapter by asking what is wrong with custodial accounting information for marketing and sales management purposes? We end by suggesting that the few observations we have been able to make in these pages underscore the need for managerial accounting information in industrial marketing and sales. With the help of the computer, there is no longer an excuse for not providing accurate, timely, managerial accounting information to marketing and sales managers.

PART FOUR

THE COMPUTER AS ASSISTANT MARKETING MANAGER

7

THE CARE AND FEEDING
OF THE CUSTOMER LIST

ALL COMPANIES HAVE CUSTOMERS

All companies have customers. Most companies try to keep a current list of customers, but only a few of the manufacturing firms we are discussing employ the customer list to greatest marketing advantage. Why? Why is it industrial marketing and sales managers do not more fully appreciate and use their own customer lists as stores of vital information about markets?

Part of the answer is many managers think they do utilize their customer lists effectively. Conventional wisdom among industrial marketers includes reference to the customer list and SIC numbers, usually within the context of "broadening the customer base." A patient listener might be rewarded with a short SIC critique, likely to conclude with the comment that the Standard Industrial Classification system as a marketing tool "may work out alright for other companies, but is too general for us."

The failure of industrial marketing and sales managers to recognize the potential marketing value of customer lists is a consequence of their failure to understand the computer's massive raw data manipulation capability. The unique information-producing capability the computer brings to industrial marketing and sales management obsoletes many notions associated with conventional marketing wisdom, and the SIC number as a general, only sometimes useful, marketing reference is one of them.

The subject of the Standard Industrial Classification system is an old one. A detailed description is omitted here for two reasons. First, much already written could not be improved upon in these pages. Second, as already mentioned, SICs have become part of conventional marketing wisdom. Most industrial marketing and sales managers are familiar with SIC numbers and how they can be used to define markets.

The problem with conventional wisdom about any subject is obsolescence. The power of the computer has placed the SIC number at the descriptive center of a company's ability to:

- [ ] Define and measure markets
- [ ] Determine relative size of markets
- [ ] Pinpoint demand
- [ ] Identify market segments
- [ ] Quantify penetration by market segment
- [ ] Track saturation by market segment
- [ ] Systematically develop lists of prospects with the same demand characteristics as customers. These are among the most highly qualified prospects a sales force can contact.

Accomplishing these objectives is the purpose of the care and feeding of the customer list.

THE CARE AND FEEDING EXERCISE

The care and feeding of the customer list presupposes highly qualified prospects for a company's products are desirable. Companies with already sufficient numbers of prospects can ignore the care and feeding exercise. Companies who view their markets as well defined, and know, or are indifferent to, relative market size and rates of penetration, can avoid the hard work associated with developing such marketing information from customer lists. Most manufacturing firms, however, are not in these categories.

At the conclusion of Chapter 4, we discussed MAP CF-1A. This MAP is a listing of customers and prospects sorted by "ship-to" address and SIC number. The list also includes "establishment size" and "customer" or "prospect" codification. MAP CF-1A is a good place to begin learning about the care and feeding exercise. The typical customer list may include (1) customer names and addresses without a "bill-to," "ship-to" breakdown; (2) zip codes, if already part of an address; and (3) SIC numbers scattered here and there. Value as a marketing tool is minimal. The care and feeding exercise involves adding a number of qualifying factors to the typical customer list. These qualifying factors are entered as attributes in the computer's CUSTOMER FILE. (See Table 7.1)

When the care and feeding exercise has been completed, the computer's massive raw data manipulation capability can be employed to sort information about markets, customers, and prospects in a number of useful ways. Marketing productivity is improved when marketing and sales managers can systematically identify, and track progress in, markets and market segments; and make decisions about highly qualified prospects they may wish contacted based on accurate, timely, information they never had before.

TABLE 7.1
Customer File Attributes—Chart of Files

0. cust#
1. name
2. bill-to address*
3. city, state
4. county*
5. zip code*
6. phone
7. purchase contact*
8. use contact*
9. sic*
10. credit
11. acct-bal
12. status
13. terms
14. via
15. ship-to address*
16. last-date
17. audit
18. tax
19. partial?
20. rep code*
21. estab. size code*
22. sales rev. code*
23. model no. code*
24. cust. code*
25. prospect code*
26.
27.

CUSTOMER FILE ATTRIBUTES

Although qualifying factors required to produce desired information reflect the needs of individual companies, Table 7.1 is presented as an example of CUSTOMER FILE attributes that might appear in the CHART OF FILES representing a computer system. Thirteen qualifying marketing and sales factors, marked by asterisks, appear as attributes in this file. Before explaining how data is developed to support the various attributes in the CUSTOMER FILE shown in Table 7.1, a brief summary of reasons why these particular file attributes were chosen is appropriate.

Although commingling customers and prospects in one file (Attributes 24 and 25) may appear strange at first, it must be remembered that the computer is impartial in this regard. MAP CF-1A is one example of what can result when customers and prospects, suitably coded, are kept in a single file. When customers and prospects, sorted by "ship-to" address, SIC number, and "establishment size" code, appear together on one list, identifications and comparisons can easily be made for purposes of conveying information, for example, to manufacturers' reps in distant sales territories. (See MAP CF-1A Commentary.)

Attributes 2 and 15 identify "bill-to" and "ship-to" addresses. Although these addresses can be the same, they often are different. The typical customer list commonly ignores this important statistical distinction. The determination of market penetration, for example, in a particular market segment, requires that customers and prospects be identified by "ship-to" or user address; a "bill-to" address is insufficient information in this regard.

The "bill-to" address is equally insufficient information for purposes of determining market potential. If Exxon is among prospective customers, and a company's products may be used at several Exxon plant locations around the country, listing Exxon's "bill-to" address or addresses in the CUSTOMER FILE fails to deal with the problem.

Attributes 7 and 8 provide names of the people who purchase and use a company's products. This information is employed in conjunction with the computer's "word-processing" capability to systematically provide managers with intelligence about markets. Marketing intelligence gathering, a largely ignored subject, is discussed in Chapter 9.

Attribute 4 identifies the county in which the customer or prospect is located. In many distributor and rep firms, sales areas are assigned by county. In the absence of specific information about prospects in each county assigned to a particular salesperson, manufacturers must rely on distributor and rep sales management for progress reports. Attribute 4 makes it possible for manufacturers to track the progress of distributor and rep salespersons whose sales assignments are not controlled by them. This attribute also facilitates statistical updating if the manufacturer assigns distributor and rep sales territories by county.

Attribute 5 is zip code information. Distributor and rep firms in metropolitan areas are often unable to assign sales areas by county. In the interest of selling efficiency, they tend to assign customers and prospects to salespersons in these areas on a geographical, zip code, basis. Attribute 5 makes it possible for manufacturers to track the progress of distributor and rep salespersons in city territories also. Zip code information facilitates periodic "cleaning" of the customer list. Sorted by zip code numbers, duplications in the CUSTOMER FILE are easily identified and removed.

Attribute 9, the SIC number, is usually four-digit. There are five-digit and seven-digit SICs available in some classifications but, for most industrial marketing and sales management purposes, the four-digit SIC, combined with qualifying factors we are discussing, is all that is needed. The four-digit SIC number is also common to external data bases that may be consulted as part of the care and feeding exercise.

Attribute 20, the rep code, identifies customers and prospects in a distributor or rep territory by the sales areas making up that territory. Demand for a company's products exists on four levels:

1. Total demand—national, international.
2. Regional demand—southern, northern, eastern, western.
3. Territorial demand—Chicago, Houston, Buffalo.
4. Area demand—salesperson C. Brown, Chicago.

Levels of demand are introduced to emphasize an important point. Marketing productivity is methodically improved in proportion to marketing and sales management's ability to allocate expenditures associated with the marketing and sales effort in the necessary product, sales territory, and customer class detail. The odds are against manufacturing companies we are discussing having accurate, updated, prospect information at the area demand level. Usually, attribute 20 is a four-digit code; as 42.04, where 42 designates the Chicago sales territory, for example, and 04 is salesperson C. Brown.

Attribute 21, establishment size, is a qualifying factor of great importance. When four-digit SICs are employed for marketing and sales management purposes without "establishment size" information, they are often too general to be useful. It is the SIC number, without explicit "establishment size" information, that explains and supports the conventional wisdom about SICs mentioned earlier.

The identification of market potential for a manufacturer's products may include, for example, SIC 2819. All establishments described by this number are involved in similar industrial activity to the extent that detail can be expressed in a four-digit classification; as such, the industry classification is usually of some value to marketing and sales managers. But companies described by SIC 2819 range in size from smallest to largest. Demand for a company's products, however, is unlikely to be equally distributed among all companies in a particular SIC category. The concentration of marketing and sales effort on the largest companies may ignore the fact that most of the market potential in a given class resides in companies *not* largest in size. The efficient allocation of marketing and sales expenditures is served by "establishment size" information regarding SICs.

"Establishment size" is size of the "ship-to" or user address. Whether expressed in terms of number of employees or sales dollars, this attribute in the CUSTOMER FILE provides an important, new, analytical dimension to the use of SICs in industrial marketing and sales management. "Establishment size" is alphabetically coded by size class. The size of individual classes may vary with individual companies and markets, but Table 7.2 presents a typical "establishment size" codification.

TABLE 7.2
Establishment Size Classification

Code	No. of Employees
A	1–49
B	50–99
C	100–499
D	500–999
E	1,000 +

Attribute 22, the sales revenue code, is the result of determining which customers, by SIC and "establishment size," make up most of company sales. Prospects having the same demand characteristics can then be appropriately coded as to sales revenue expectation. As an example, all customers in SIC and "establishment size" classes making up the first 80 percent of sales are designated by a "1" in Attribute 22; all prospects in these classes are also designated "1." Customers in SIC and "establishment size" classes comprising the next 15 percent of sales are designated by a "2," and all prospects in these classes are similarly designated. Customers and prospects in the last 5 percent of sales are designated by a "3" in this attribute. Such sales revenue ranking further qualifies marketing and sales priorities regarding prospects to be contacted.

Although Attribute 22 is volatile, with some SIC and "establishment size" classes changing rank from one operating period to the next, it can be an important source of information for marketing and sales managers intent upon improving marketing productivity.

Attribute 23, model number, is coded to accommodate the marketing needs of manufacturers. If a company markets a few products to many different customer classes, this attribute may be coded by application. Companies that market relatively many products to a few customer classes may employ a product or model number code. Those companies marketing only a few products to a few customer classes might not use this attribute at all.

Before explaining how data to support customer file attributes is developed, and how the customer list is employed to identify highly qualified prospects, it is interesting to compare a section of a customer list *before* and *after* the care and feeding exercise.

With reference to Table 7.3, it is likely a company as large as BASF in Geismer, La., would have been known as a good prospect for this company's products or services before the care and feeding exercise. But it is unlikely a manager could keep in mind the similarities between customers and prospects in regard to SIC, establishment size, sales revenue, and product application. Any one of these similarities, once recalled, might trigger an action that turns a good prospect into a good customer. Table 7.3 presents information about one customer and one prospect. We would anticipate many more prospects as a result of the care and feeding of the customer list.

An external data base will provide the prospect's name, "ship-to" address, zip code, SIC number, and establishment size by number of employees or sales dollars. The remainder of editing and

TABLE 7.3
Customer List Care and Feeding—Before and After

		Customer List—Before			
Cust.	Addr.	City	State	Zip	
Hooker Chem.	180 'B' St.	Niag. Falls	NY	14302	
		- No Prospects -			

	"Ship-to"				Customer and Prospect List—After						
Cust.	Addr.	City	Cty	St	Zip	SIC	Size	Rev.	Model	Rep	C-P
Hooker Chem.	11 Elm St.	Niag. Falls	Niag.	NY	14302	2812	E	1	540	38.01	C
BASF	6 Trimble Rd.	Geismer		LA	70754	2812	D	1	540	16.04	P

coding work is done internally by marketing and sales department personnel.

The information provided by an external data base may be entered into the CUSTOMER FILE on magnetic tape. However, it is marketing and sales department personnel who will provide the codification of "establishment size" we have discussed. It is also those same individuals who will enter, as attributes in the CUSTOMER FILE, rep, sales revenue, model number or application, and customer or prospect codes.

DEVELOPING DATA TO SUPPORT CUSTOMER FILE ATTRIBUTES

Developing the data needed to support attributes in the CUSTOMER FILE is hard work. For a manufacturing company with a customer list of over a few hundred names and addresses, there is the problem of managing extensive clerical detail. Also, this problem is usually complicated by an absence of available staff.

The most advanced computer-based information system will not automatically supply and enter the data required. The editing and coding part of the exercise is manual, and can seem to be endless. Energy, zeal, and dedication to possibilities that follow completion of the task are a requirement if the effort is to be successful. The caveat about "roads paved with good intentions" is particularly applicable in this regard.

Still, as we have tried to emphasize in these pages, the potential payoff is large. It is not unusual for companies with lists of customers numbering in the hundreds to identify highly qualified prospects numbering in the thousands as a result of the care and feeding exercise. The customer base may be broadened as a consequence, without introduction of new products. Despite difficulty involved, the effort usually proves worthwhile.

Advice about organizing to accomplish this work is direct and simple. One person should be made responsible for the care and feeding exercise, and regarded as performing a task of vital importance to the company, and marketing and sales management. Here, in summary form, is what must be done:

1. *Verify the roster of all customers who have purchased products currently for sale.* If a division of the company.was sold a few years ago, eliminate customers for the division's products from the list. A re-

view of sales order files, paid invoices, quality control records, and the service and repair log may be necessary in order that a total customer list is assured.

2. *Distinguish between "bill-to" and "ship-to" addresses.* Although sales order forms usually make this distinction, it is not observed on the typical customer list. "Bill-to" and "ship-to" addresses are both statistically important, but emphasis should be placed on producing a complete, correctly identified, "ship-to" customer list.

3. *Identify each customer by SIC number.* The basis of the four-digit SIC system is described in the Standard Industrial Classification Manual, a government publication. Five-digit and seven-digit SIC numbers are contained in the Census of Manufactures, also available from the U.S. Government Printing Office in Washington, D.C. Another valuable SIC identification source are the volumes of credit information published by Dun and Bradstreet.

Because an external data base such as Dun and Bradstreet's will be necessary in order that a country-wide market profile can be extrapolated from the SIC identifications made on the customer list, a Dun and Bradstreet sales representative may be able to arrange for credit information volumes to be borrowed, while SIC idenifications are made, should the company not subscribe to the Dun and Bradstreet credit service.

Information about the Dun and Bradstreet market identifier service is as close as the reader's telephone, so it will not be described in detail here. This service, and other similar services, have for many years made available information about companies of interest to marketers. In the case of Dun and Bradstreet, the information is a by-product of the financial and credit reportage they do. SIC numbers and "establishment size" are two items of the information.

Identifying customers by SIC number requires that a judgment be made when more than one SIC number is used to describe a company's industrial activities. Multiple SICs are commonly associated with large corporations where several operating divisions may exist. The task of selecting among alternative SICs is made easier by SIC specificity at the four-digit level of detail. The objective is to determine the SIC number describing a company's industrial activity at a "ship-to" address. Assignment of correct SIC numbers to the "ship-to" customer list may be expected to be readily completed after source volumes are obtained.

4. *Identify each customer by "establishment size."* The determination of "establishment size," or size at the "ship-to" address, may

be complicated by a lack of published information. Dun and Brad-street, for example, provides "establishment size" information as a feature of its market identifier service, but only for establishments contacted as part of the Dun and Bradstreet financial and credit re-port activities. Manufacturers whose markets include "ship-to" ad-dresses where there is no finance or accounting function must rely on their own salespeople and field representatives for "establishment size," as well as other customer information.

While the SIC number must be exact to at least four digits, "es-tablishment size" need not be exact to the last employee or sales dol-lar. The "establishment size" codification, as already mentioned, is by class.

5. *Look for SIC and "establishment size" patterns.* Typically, a pattern of SIC numbers will emerge as identification of the "ship-to" customer list is completed. What may first appear to be discrete four-digit SIC numbers, for example, will be found to have the first two digits in common. Much useful market information may be obtained by study of the patterns of industry classification as they relate to a company's products or services. In this sense, the care and feeding exercise is a fishing expedition. Among many possibilities:

a. Which SIC numbers *not* part of the present customer list re-veal a possible industry relationship with listed SICs?

b. Do "establishment size" classifications by SIC indicate many customers of different sizes, or are present customers mainly large companies?

c. What reasons can be given to encourage or discourage the idea that unlisted SICs represent market potential?

d. What reasons can be given to encourage or discourage the idea that companies other than large companies, or com-panies of different "establishment size" than listed, repre-sent market potential?

e. How may possibilities be checked before money is spent on a market profile of these SIC and "establishment size" pat-terns?

f. If a company markets products through industrial distribu-tors and manufacturers' reps, are some prospective cus-tomers ignored by these independent agents because they are too small, distant, or have other supply needs the dis-tributor or rep does not serve?

g. Will other distribution channels be required if sales contact with these prospects is to be made?

Meetings held to discuss such questions and related subjects often represent a company's first systematic attempts to define and measure markets. The SIC and "establishment size" classifications of interest, both listed and unlisted, form the basis for the market profile.

6. *Order the market profile.* The market profile is an extrapolation from SIC and "establishment size" identifications made as part of the care and feeding of the customer list. It will list, usually by county or state, all companies in the market identifier base in SIC and "establishment size" classifications of interest to the user. Because these classifications either describe actual customers, or companies in industrial classifications related to those of actual customers, the market profile is a listing of *prospects* with demand characteristics the same as, or similar to, *customers*. There are no more highly qualified prospects for a company's products or services.

a. If SIC 2812 is part of a customer list identification, how many companies identified by SIC 2812, in the "establishment size" classes of interest, exist in the marketing universe?

b. Where are they located? How many are customers? How many are prospects?

c. Are all prospects being contacted? By whom?

d. Is the ratio of customers to prospects approximately the same for all sales areas?

e. Which sales areas have better customer to prospect ratios than others? Why?

f. What is present status with prospects?

g. What are the reasons these prospects have not become customers?

h. Have they purchased from a competitor? When and why?

Some prospects identified in a market profile will, for various reasons, be eliminated from the prospect list. If the care and feeding exercise has been properly done, however, many highly qualified prospect names and addresses will be keyed into the computer.

There are administrative decisions to be made in regard to the market profile that are too numerous to discuss here. Detail can be confusing. In general, however, market identifier service representatives are knowledgeable and willing explainers of alternatives available and guidelines to be observed. Market profiles, when accurate, complete, and regularly updated, make informed and methodical approaches to the allocation of sales effort possible. Increased operating efficiency, steady sales and profit growth, and improved marketing productivity are the result.

7. *Complete the codification of* CUSTOMER FILE *attributes.* Market profiles we have been discussing provide the following information in support of CUSTOMER FILE attributes:

a. company name
b. "ship-to" address
c. city, state, zip code, county
d. phone
e. SIC number
f. establishment size (number of employees or sales dollars)

Marketing and sales department personnel involved in the care and feeding exercise must provide the following information if identification is to be complete:

g. "bill-to" addresses
h. establishment size code
i. rep code
j. sales revenue code
k. model number or application code
l. customer code
m. prospect code
n. purchase and use contacts.

The work associated with keying these attributes into the CUSTOMER FILE can be avoided if the assumption on which the care and feeding exercise is based is denied. The care and feeding of the customer list assumes that firms of similar size in homogeneous industry groupings share demand for products or services more or less equally. The assumption is a large one, ignoring the influence of competitive offerings, customer prejudice, unique circumstances, and differences in the ability of salespeople.

The decision to do nothing, however, in the face of the inevitable ambiguities, exceptions, and hard work, rests on an assumption equally large. That assumption is that the care and feeding exercise is useless and that all the companies competing in an industry will also choose to ignore its possibilities. We have seen patience and determination in regard to the demands of the care and feeding exercise generously rewarded many times.

Earlier, it was mentioned that successful completion of the care and feeding exercise, and the massive raw data manipulation capability of the computer, make it possible for information about customers and prospects to be sorted in many useful ways. This chapter concludes by making an important distinction between the computer's sorting capability and MAPs.

The computer can be programmed to sort in many ways. But sorting is costly, involving various quantities of programming and machine time. All sorting is not equally useful to managers. For this reason, we prefer to concentrate on MAPs. MAPs are sortings, or depend on sortings, that enhance decision-making. For marketing and sales management purposes, MAPs are the highest expression of the computer's unique informational product.

What updated detail, presently unknown to marketing and sales managers, would contribute to decisions that increase operating efficiency and improve marketing productivity? Although there are many MAP possibilities, examples of MAPs common to most industrial marketing and sales management activities are presented in the next chapter.

8

SELECTED MAPs—NEW ROADS TO SALES AND PROFITS

Marketing Application Programs (MAPs) are, in one sense, no different than other application programs. Any use to which the computer is put to provide information involves application programs. However, all application programs do not have the same value to managers interested in increasing operating efficiency and improving marketing productivity. Sorting customers alphabetically, for example, provides no information to enhance management decision-making. Sales analysis listing salespeople who have exceeded forecast or quota provides no important decision-making information.

For marketing and sales management purposes, MAPs are the highest expression of the computer's unique informational product when they make managers aware of something that has been hidden in the past for lack of real information. MAPs that provide real information that can be used to influence results not otherwise obtainable are the MAPs most useful to industrial marketing and sales managers. They are the MAPs this book is about. They are as informationally versatile as the power of managerial imagination and the user's computer system. Their design and development can present problems, so the following caveats are appropriate.

The important MAPs make the previously unapparent (for lack of real information) obvious to managers. There is no facile approach to their creation. Patience and careful thought are required. The participant in the design and development of these MAPs, however, will find the creative process self-generating. As with any craft, this one is learned by doing.

It is a good rule to keep MAPs simple and run many of them, rather than design complicated MAPs that may unnecessarily burden programming and machine capacities. Although an idea often contradicted by computer specialists, all MAPs need not emerge complete on a computer print-out. For example, MAP SF-1A is the result of a hand tabulation based on a computerized array of orders not shown here. Because this particular MAP needed to be updated only every six months or so, a two-step approach saved programming costs and was the least cost method of obtaining the information.

The MAPs presented here are meant to be examples of some of the many MAP possibilities that exist. Because computer print-outs have a way of fast dissolving into a wash of black and white, each MAP is presented with commentary on the facing page.

SELECTED MAPs

MAP QF-1A

Commentary

A subjective probability of bookings' success, or S.P., is assigned by sales managers and reps to each of the quotes, in total outstanding quotations in the quotation file, expected to close during a particular month;—in this instance, October 1979. As discussed in Chapter 4, this is a method of further assuring the integrity of the master schedule. In companies where quotations are regularly made as part of pre-sale activity, and where production schedules do not always reflect firm orders, this MAP reduces costly guesswork by bringing the bookings' horizon closer to the master schedule.

The gross value of outstanding quotations expected to close during the month is $490,384; net expected value, after probabilities are applied, is $293,042. Note that, of sixteen quotations expected to close, seven are considered to have a 100 percent chance of being booked. They total $156,960. They reduce by that amount the uncertainty with which we are trying to deal. The value reflects unbooked orders that salespeople know have been awarded, or feel certain will be awarded.

Note also that six different products are represented in closing quotations, with the possibility of a seventh the result of a qualifying digit (4425-1 and 4425-2). S.P. associated with each product type ranges from certainty to .25. The task of predetermining unit amounts and product types to be added to the master schedule from anticipated, one-month, quotation closings is correspondingly facilitated.

MAP QF-1A

QUOTE CLOSE - 10.79
S.P.

CUSTOMER	ADDRESS	REP	UNITS	QUOTES PART NO	$TOTAL	S.P.	UNITS	NET $TOTAL
Amer-T	Dallas	34.04	24	7315-2	28,410	100	24	28,410
Auto. Cont.	L.A.	52.01	6	6420-1	60,804	50	3	30,402
AVC	L.A.	52.01	48	7315-2	56,820	50	24	28,410
Cook Co	N.J.	12.06	10	8420-1	25,000	100	10	25,000
COPA	Houston	34.10	6	7315-2	7,100	50	3	3,550
Dorico	Houston	34.08	100	5090	84,400	25	25	21,100
Fuelco	Boston	09.01	6	7315-2	6,800	100	6	6,800
Gamma Inc.	Phila.	16.04	12	5090	9,950	100	12	9,950
Gray Mfg.	Detroit	21.02	3	6420-1	29,800	100	3	29,800
Hilbert	N. Orleans	33.06	20	4425-1	40,000	50	10	20,000
Humco	Denver	48.02	10	7315-2	9,900	80	8	7,920
Montco	Denver	48.02	6	7315-2	6,400	50	3	3,200
Price	Cleve.	19.01	8	4425-1	18,000	50	4	9,000
So. Union	El Paso	30.03	6	4425-2	12,000	100	6	12,000
Thermco	Chicago	22.04	20	8420-1	50,000	25	5	12,500
United	Tulsa	36.01	15	4222-4	45,000	100	15	45,000
					T-$490,384			$293,042

MAP QF-2A

Commentary

Where quotations are an important pre-sale activity, monthly quotation summaries can provide useful information for marketing and sales management purposes. A computer quotation file, into which all quotation activity is entered, furnishes the data summarized in MAP QF-2A.

It may interest managers to realize that, on a FYTD basis, the company has won about one quotation out of every four quotations made. Put another way, bookings from quotations have required about three quotation dollars to produce one bookings' dollar during the current year. How does this compare with FYTD quotation results a year ago? What would breakdowns of quotation activity in sales territories within the sales regions, and sales areas within the sales territories, reveal? This analysis introduces the idea of quotation "capture rates," the subject of MAP QF-3A, MAP QF-4A, and MAP QF-5A.

The average value of quotations outstanding this year is 40 percent higher than last year. Do a few large quotations explain this, or is there some other reason for the increase? Is it a reason management can exploit to the greater advantage of the company?

Quotation activity is costly. If this company wrote no more quotations, but improved its capture rate to one bookings' dollar for every two quotation dollars, it would increase bookings from quotations by 50 percent.

Monthly Quotation Summary
Sept. 1979

SEPTEMBER SUMMARY		QUANTITY	AMOUNT
New quotes		52	$639,792
Won quotes		(16)	(221,958)
Lost quotes		(2)	(24,624)
SEPTEMBER NEW QUOTES			
Northeast region		16	252,630
Southeast region		8	98,712
Central region		19	162,434
Western region		9	126,016
	Total	52	$639,792
OUTSTANDING QUOTES			
Northeast region		48	685,324
Southeast region		32	512,819
Central region		65	821,098
Western region		67	949,512
	Total	212	$2,968,753
FYTD SUMMARY			
9/30/78 Outstanding		182	$1,847,614
Plus: New quotes, FYTD		677	8,458,865
Less: Won quotes, FYTD		(228)	(3,418,392)
Lost quotes, FYTD		(419)	(3,919,334)
9/30/79 Outstanding		212	$2,968,753

MAP QF-3A

Commentary

The company quotation capture rate is 26.5 percent; approximately a quotation won for every four quotations made. Although different quotation capture rates are to be expected among sales regions, MAP QF-3A provides information that may be of interest to managers.

Company products are sold to all regions. List prices are the same in all regions. Good customers and prospects exist in all regions. Why is the capture rate in the Southeast region nearly double the capture rate in the Central region? If the quotation capture rate in the Central region were the same as the average capture rate of the other regions (about 30 percent), the company would have won twenty-seven more quotes. At an average quotation value of $14,000, FYTD bookings from quotations would be increased by $378,000, or 11 percent.

It is unlikely that managers planning the sales future of the Central region would systematically deal with attempts to improve the region's quotation capture rate without the relative capture rate information provided by this MAP.

MAP QF-3A

Quotation ''Capture Rate'' Summary
FYTD, Sept. 30, 1979

FYTD SUMMARY	TOTAL	NORTHEAST	SOUTHEAST	CENTRAL	WESTERN
9/30/78 Outstanding	182	54	25	60	43
New quotes, FYTD	<u>677</u>	<u>212</u>	<u>118</u>	<u>200</u>	<u>147</u>
Total quotations	859	266	143	260	190
Won quotes, FYTD	228	64	52	51	61
Quotation capture rate	26.5%	24.1%	36.4%	19.6%	32.1%

MAP QF-4A

Commentary

MAPs QF-3A, QF-4A, and QF-5A illustrate the power of the computer's massive raw data manipulation capability to provide extensively detailed quotation information to managers in an accurate and timely manner. As mentioned several times in this book, such detail is beyond the capability of manual systems in most manufacturing companies.

MAP QF-4A is a territorial breakdown of FYTD quotation activity in the Northeast region. The logic employed in analyzing the regional summary in MAP QF-3A is equally valid here. Why are quotation capture rates in 07, 14, and 19 sales territories more than double the capture rates in the other territories?

If the quotation capture rates in 04 and 21 sales territories were the same as the average capture rate of the 07, 14, and 19 sales territories (about 33 percent), the Northeast region would have won twenty-five more quotations, an increase of thirty-nine percent in Won quotes, FYTD. On the basis of average quotation value in the Northeast region, nearly $350,000 would have been added to bookings.

MAP QF-4A

Quotation ''Capture Rate'' Summary
Northeast Region
FYTD, Sept. 30, 1979

FYTD SUMMARY	TOTAL	SALES TERRITORY NO.				
		04	07	14	19	21
9/30/78 Outstanding	54	17	6	9	14	8
New quotes, FYTD	<u>212</u>	<u>82</u>	<u>28</u>	<u>43</u>	<u>30</u>	<u>29</u>
Total quotations	266	99	34	52	44	37
Won quotes, FYTD	64	15	11	18	14	6
Quotation capture rate	24.1%	15.2%	32.4%	34.6%	31.8%	16.2%

MAP QF-5A

Commentary

MAP QF-5A discloses quotation capture rates at the least common denominator of quotation activity—the individual sales areas comprising a sales territory. Sales territory 04 is a large metropolitan territory in the Northeast region. Five salespeople call on customers and prospects in the territory. It is interesting to note that half the new quotes in the territory were written by one salesperson. Two-thirds of quotations won were closed by the same salesperson. What reasons can be found to explain this? What steps can be taken to improve quotation performance in the other sales areas?

The quotation capture rate in sales territory 04 is a little better than half the national average. Why? Is there unusual competitive pressure in this territory not apparent in other sales territories? Or do these salespeople need further training in quotation reply and follow-up?

MAP QF-5A

Quotation ''Capture Rate'' Summary
Sales Territory 04
FYTD, Sept. 30, 1979

FYTD SUMMARY	TOTAL	04.01	04.02	04.03	04.04	04.05
			SALES AREA NO.			
9/30/78 Outstanding	17	8	2	0	4	3
New quotes, FYTD	82	41	17	3	10	11
Total quotations	99	49	19	3	14	14
Won quotes, FYTD	15	10	2	0	3	0
Quotation capture rate	15.2%	20.4%	10.5%	0	21.4%	0

MAP QF-6A

Commentary

The MAP fragment that is the subject of this commentary is one page of a longer computer print-out, identifying lost quotations by rep salespersons, customer quoted, SIC and "establishment size," model quoted, amount quoted, the competitor "lost-to," and the reason for the loss. A computer quotation file, into which all quotation activity is entered, furnishes the data summarized in MAP QF-6A.

Analysis of lost quotations, in sufficient detail, provides managers with information of great value in the systematic improvement of quotation performance. Similar analysis of quotations won (not shown here) would also provide useful information to managers.

<u>MAP QF-6A</u>   06:03:23   30 Sept. 1979

Lost Quotation Analysis
Sales Territory 04
FYTD, Sept. 30, 1979

REP. NO.	QUOTE NO.	CUST.	SIC-SIZE	MODEL NO.	AM'T	LOST-TO	REASON
04.01	6275	Dupont	2824 E	4425-1	$60,520	Dic.	Price
04.01	6312	Inmont	2851 D	4425-2	$44,326	Dic.	Price
04.01	6391	Herc.	2861 E	4425-1	$80,150	Dic.	Price
04.01	6411	Union Cars	2869 E	4425-1	$48,500	Dic.	Price
04.01	6438	Seton	3111 C	7315-2	$ 2,750	Sc.	Spec.
04.01	6495	Englehard	3339 D	8420-1	$ 8,800	Sc.	Price
04.01	6507	Clark	3536 B	4224-4	$ 1,875	Dic.	Price
04.01	6618	Berkman	3674 B	5090	$ 5,900	Bach.	Spec.

MAP CF-1A

Commentary

The customer list is a repository of vital marketing information in several respects. This subject is discussed in Chapter 7. The MAP fragment that is the subject of this commentary is one page of a longer computer print-out, identifying customers and prospects by four-digit SIC and establishment size.

The company's customer list was originally identified by four-digit SIC; and "establishment size" or number of employees at the "ship to" address. On the basis of the identifications, an extrapolation was made which became a prospect list. The customer list and prospect list were merged in the customer file, and individual customer names and prospect names designated "C" or "P." Establishment size was arbitrarily coded, alphabetically, according to class size; in this case A through E. Methods employed are explained in Chapter 7.

Of nineteen SIC identifications in the twenty-eight series on this page, nine are listed as prospects. We note with interest that while Hooker Chemical is a customer in Niagara Falls, N.Y., BASF Wyandotte in Geismar, La., a plant nearly as large and in the same SIC classification, remains a prospect. The logic that states that a prime prospect is a production plant or establishment, identified according to the same industry characteristics as present customers, applies to all the prospects designated on this page.

<u>MAP CF-1A</u>   05:10:53   28 Sept. 1979

Ship-to-Cust. Prosp. List
by SIC#, Estab. Size

SIC	ESTAB. SIZE	CUST	C-P	CITY
2812	E	Hooker Chemical	C	Niagara Falls, N.Y. 14302
2812	D	BASF Wyandotte	P	Geismar, LA 70734
2816	C	Celanese	C	Pasadena, TX 77505
2816	C	Celanese	P	Charlotte, NC 28210
2818	E	Tenn. East.	C	Kingsport, TX 37662
2819	A	Cities Service	C	Blackwell, OK 74631
2819	A	Cities Service	P	Cheney, KS 67025
2819	A	Cities Service	C	Longview, TX 75601
2819	A	Coulton Chemical	P	Oregon, OH 43616
2819	D	Martin Marietta	P	Charlotte, NC 28214
2819	D	Amer. Cyanamid	C	Willow Island, WV 26190
2821	E	Dow Corning	C	Midland, MI 48640
2821	B	Conoco	C	Oklahoma City, OK 73115
2821	B	Diamond Shamrock	C	Amarillo, TX 79106
2821	C	Diamond Shamrock	P	Redwood City, CA 94063
2821	C	FMC Corp.	P	Modesto, CA 95352
2821	C	FMC Corp.	P	Westvaco, N.Y. 82935
2821	C	Diamond Shamrock	C	Ashtabula, OH 44004
2821	C	Dow Corning	P	Hemlock, MI 48626

MAP CF-2A

Commentary

MAP CF-2A results from analysis of the FYTD customer list in terms of customer classes that make up the most of sales. The bookings' figures were arrayed by computer in a supporting sales order file print-out (not shown here), largest-to-smallest, according to customer "ship-to" address.

The analysis of the customer list, indicating by SIC and "establishment size" class those customers making up most of total sales, should include all orders associated with customer classes of interest, not merely large orders. There is no hard and fast analytical approach to this. Ultimately, analysis should determine those customer classes that represent the core of FYTD bookings.

In this case, the ten customer classes designated sales revenue code "1" in MAP CF-2A comprise about 50 percent of total sales. The eleven customer classes designated sales revenue code "2" represent about 30 percent of total sales. MAP CF-2A identifies, among hundreds of customer classes on the FYTD customer list, twenty-one customer classes that make up 80 percent of sales.

The idea is to identify prospects with the same SIC and "establishment size" characteristics as core customers. Such identification is the subject of MAP CF-3A.

Customers by Rev. Code, SIC, Estab. Size
FYTD, May 31, 1979

REVENUE CODE	SIC	ESTAB. SIZE
1	1311	D
1	1311	E
1	1629	D
1	2851	D
1	2851	E
1	2861	E
1	3511	D
1	3511	E
1	3823	C
1	8911	E
2	1711	B
2	1711	C
2	2611	C
2	2813	B
2	2819	C
2	2819	D
2	2821	D
2	4612	B
2	4922	B
2	4923	B
2	4924	C

MAP CF-3A

Commentary

MAP CF-3A, as shown, is a page fragment of a long computer print-out. The computer was programmed to sort for prospects identified by specific SIC and "establishment size" classes. These identifications were the result of an analysis of the customer list indicating, by SIC and "establishment size" class, those customers making up most of total sales. The largest customer classes, and prospects with the same SIC and "establishment size" characteristics, are assigned a sales revenue code of "1." The next largest customer and prospect classes are assigned a sales revenue code of "2" or "3."

MAP CF-3A reveals that in the Chicago sales territory, in sales area 42.04, there are four prospects with SIC and "establishment size" characteristics in sales revenue code "2" on the customer list. This means that many of the company's customers are described by these SIC and "establishment size" classes. The computer's massive raw data manipulation capability makes possible a cross-fertilization of SIC and "establishment size" information of great value to managers.

Why has this company sold to many 4924C customers across the country, but not to prospects in the 42.04 sales area with the same identifying characteristics? How about the 2813B prospects —Have they purchased from a competitor? Why?

<u>MAP CF-3A</u> 03:41:47 10 June 1979

Prospects by Cust. SIC, Estab. Size, Rev. Code

REP#	PROSPECT	ADDRESS	CITY	SIC-SIZE	REV. CODE
42.04	No. Ill. Gas	750 N. Elmhurst	Arlington Hts.	4924C	2
42.04	No. Ill. Gas	615 Eastern	Bellwood	4924C	2
42.04	Liquid Carb.	2000 W. Dolton	Calumet City	2813B	2
42.04	Chemetron Corp.	111 E. Wacker Dr.	Chicago	2813B	2

MAP CF-4A

Commentary

The company's customer list was originally identified by four-digit
SIC, and "establishment size" or number of employees at the
"ship-to" address. Establishment size was arbitrarily coded, alphabetically, according to class size. On the basis of the identifications, an extrapolation was made that became a prospect list.
Methods employed are explained in Chapter 7.

Although MAP CF-4A summarizes only customers and prospects contained in the customer classes presented in MAP CF-2A,
there is no reason why total customers and prospects should not be
summarized for every customer class comprising the company's
marketing universe.

Knowing the extent to which company products occupy market segments, and the extent of market saturation evidenced by
the number of prospects known to have purchased competitive
products, can be useful information to marketing and sales
managers.

MAP CF-4A

Total Customers and Prospects by Customer Class
May 1979

SIC	ESTAB. SIZE	CLASS TOTAL	CUSTOMERS	PROSPECTS
1311	D	23	11	12
1311	E	14	9	5
1629	D	18	5	13
2851	D	26	14	12
2851	E	12	6	6
2861	E	8	3	5
3511	D	67	20	47
3511	E	21	8	13
3823	C	88	18	70
8911	E	10	5	5
1711	B	226	32	194
1711	C	115	21	94
2611	C	73	18	55
2813	B	105	29	76
2819	C	69	19	50
2819	D	18	6	12
2821	D	20	6	14
4612	B	142	11	131
4922	B	95	31	64
4923	B	82	17	65
4924	C	44	15	29

MAP CF-5A

Commentary

Although the twenty-one SIC and "establishment size" classes shown here represent core customers, many other potential prospect identifications may exist by virtue of different, perhaps related, SIC numbers as well as other "establishment size" classes within the same SIC number. Nevertheless, having a statistical summary by sales territory of customers and prospects within core customer classes provides useful information to marketing and sales managers.

The total number of core customers revealed in MAP CF-4A is 304, 23.8 percent of class totals. The total number of core customers in sales area 34.01, 13, is relatively much higher after adjustment for core customer classes not represented there. At the same time, the number of prospects far exceeds the number of customers in both instances—a matter of interest to managers involved.

Chapter 7 mentioned that the power of the computer has placed the SIC number at the descriptive center of a company's ability to define and measure markets, determine relative size of markets, and pinpoint demand. MAP CF-5A is a good example of how this capability might be applied to a sales area.

Rev. Code 1, 2, Customers and Prospects by Cust. Class
Sales Territory 34

34.01	REV. CODE	SIC	ESTAB. SIZE	CLASS TOTAL	CUSTOMERS	PROSPECTS
	1	1311	D	3	0	3
	1	1311	E	2	1	1
	1	1629	D	4	1	3
	1	2851	D	0	0	0
	1	2851	E	0	0	0
	1	2861	E	0	0	0
	1	3511	D	6	2	4
	1	3511	E	2	1	1
	1	3823	C	0	0	0
	1	8911	E	4	3	1
	2	1711	B	12	2	10
	2	1711	C	5	1	4
	2	2611	C	0	0	0
	2	2813	B	0	0	0
	2	2819	C	8	2	6
	2	2819	D	2	0	2
	2	2821	D	0	0	0
	2	4612	B	0	0	0
	2	4922	B	0	0	0
	2	4923	B	0	0	0
	2	4924	C	0	0	0
				T. 48	13	35

MAP SF-1A

Commentary

Total FYTD bookings in period comparisons are up by $1,200K; an impressive 39 percent. Rate of real bookings' growth, because of price increases, is 30 percent; but the totals conceal important information.

Order classification in this MAP is arbitrary. The grouping of order classes above and below $25K is arbitrary, involving other analytical considerations. The bookings' figures were arrayed by computer in a supporting sales order file print-out not presented here; largest-to-smallest, according to customer "ship to" address, a subject discussed in Chapter 7. Comparisons are revealing.

Of ten order classes, numbered in the far left column, two (numbers 1 and 4) represent 105 percent of the total increase in bookings, indicating performance in some other classes is down. These are numbers 2, 5, and 6, where 1979 bookings, adjusted for the price increases, are down nearly $400K when compared to 1978. Order classes 7, 8, 9, and 10, after adjustments for price increases, are either slightly up, or slightly down in 1979. In view of impressive total bookings' growth, we note with interest that seven of ten order classes are either relatively unchanged or sharply down. We additionally observe that, during FYTD 1979, 30 of 691 total orders booked represented over 60 percent of total dollar bookings; also that about half of all booked orders make up 3 percent of total dollar volume.

Order Value Analysis
U.S. Bookings, FYTD-9 Months
1979 vs. 1978

ORDER VALUE CLASS		1979				1978		
	NO	%-T	$TOTALS	%-T	NO	%-T	$TOTALS	%-T
1. $100K+	5		$1,340K		3		$390K	
2. 75-99.9	4		476		5		620	
3. 50-74.9	3		198		2		107	
4. 25-49.9	18		702		10		391	
Sub-T	30	4.3%	$2,716K	63.3%	20	3.1%	$1,508K	48.8%
5. $15-24.9K	18		$288K		20		$328K	
6. 10-14.9	12		180		25		282	
7. 5-9.9	62		430		62		390	
8. 2-4.9	110		364		106		344	
9. 1-1.9	105		174		85		128	
Sub-T	307	44.5%	$1,436K	33.5%	298	45.4%	$1,472K	47.7%
10. <$1K	354	51.2%	$136K	3.2%	338	51.5%	108K	3.5%
T	691	100.0%	$4,288K	100.0%	656	100.0%	$3,088K	100.0%

MAP SF-2A

Commentary

It was stated in Chapter 4 that the measurement of market penetration for management purposes doesn't mean much unless market segments are also identified and measured. MAP SF-1A provides information about the number and relative size of orders booked in two operating periods. MAP SF-2A shows the market segments involved in
the largest of these bookings.

As discussed in Chapter 7, the Standard Industrial Classification (SIC) takes on new significance when accompanied by "establishment size" codification. Were the three largest orders booked during the first nine months of 1978 one-time orders? Or have quotations in the 4612 and 4922 SIC classifications been lost to competitors during 1979? Why?

Note some of the new SIC classifications that appear in large orders booked during 1979. Where did 8911, 1311, 1629, and 5087 come from? Are there more of these SIC numbers identified in quotations outstanding? Are these new market segments for the company? Why?

MAP SF-2A

Market Segment Analysis
Large Orders,
U.S. Bookings,
FYTD-9 months
1979 vs. 1978

ORDER CLASS	NO.	1979 $ TOTALS	SIC	NO.	1978 $ TOTALS	SIC
1. $100K+	5	$1,340K	1311E	3	$390K	4922D
			8911E			4612C
			1629E			2816D
			2821D			
			3511D			
2. $75-99.9	4	476K	8911E	5	620K	2816D
			1311E			2819D
			1629C			3511C
			5087C			4612C
						4922B
3. $50-74.9	3	198K	4922B	2	107K	4922B
			4612C			4612C
			2824D			

MAP SF-3A

Commentary

In manufacturing companies where products are marketed through distributors and reps, MAP SF-3A provides updated FYTD sales detail which can be useful to marketing and sales managers. In this manufacturing company, there are 120 rep salespeople working in sales areas in the U.S. and Canada. There are 2,400 "ship-to" customer addresses, and over 12,000 prospects. MAP SF-3A is one page of a computer print-out listing total FYTD customers by region, rep salesperson, and order amount.

We note with interest the large difference in FYTD customers and order amounts among the three rep salespeople listed. Ten rep salespeople call on customers and prospects in all of sales territory 34. Marketing mix expenditures are spread across all ten sales areas. Prospects exist in all sales areas. Marketing productivity suggests that satisfactory results be obtained in all sales areas.

In this case, the fiscal year is half over. Sales area 34.02 includes some of the company's largest customers. Only one has purchased so far this year. Why? Has there been quotation activity? Have quotations been lost? Why? The complete print-out of FYTD sales results in territory 34 indicates the contribution made to the total by individual rep salespersons. Comparisons can then be made with prospects identified in each sales area, quotation activity in each sales area, and FYTD results obtained a year ago in each sales area.

FYTD Ship-to Cust. List by Region, Rep#, Order Am'T.

REP #	CUSTOMERS	ADDRESS	CITY, STATE	ORDER AMOUNT
34.01	C&R Labs	600 36th St.	McAllen, TX	$ 5,260
34.01	Brown & Rowe	4100 Clinton Dr.	Houston, TX	18,110
34.01	Celanese	Hwy. 77	Bishop, TX	1,200
34.01	Hudson Eng.	5925 Mills Blvd.	Houston, TX	120,950
34.01	Wel-Lab, Inc.	16 Holly Rd.	Alice, TX	2,720
			Total	$148,240
34.02	Alcoa	Hwy. 20	Parkdale, TX	$ 900
34.02	AMOCO	E. 8th St.	Tyler, TX	1,200
34.02	AMOCO	802 Drake Ave.	Edgewood, TX	750
34.02	ARCO Eng.	1200 Grand St.	Dallas, TX	2,375
34.02	Cities Serv.	P.O. Box 372	Canton, TX	2,100
34.02	Johnson Cont.	542 Park	Carrollton, TX	96
34.02	Midcont. Supply	P.O. Box 954	Ft. Worth, TX	192
34.02	Omni Eng.	Meridian, WY	Ft. Worth, TX	192
34.02	Sedco	3062 Jethro Blvd.	Dallas, TX	4,200
34.02	TEXACO	1400 W. 1st St.	Wichita Falls, TX	14,150
34.02	Tex. Util. Fuel	Hwy 179	Teague, TX	96
			Total	$26,251
34.03	Foster Wheeler	Orange Wks.	Orange, TX	$ 192
			Total $	192

9

MARKETING INTELLIGENCE GATHERING

It was said in Chapter 3 that the right information for industrial marketing and sales managers is real information. Real information is new information, and is only obtained by asking the right questions. The MAPs discussed in Chapter 8 result from questions asked in order to generate new information about marketing and sales management activities. The source of this information is a manufacturing company's own data base. MAPs produce internal information.

Any information helping marketing and sales managers to make decisions that improve a company's competitive position is Marketing intelligence. Although sources of such information may be internal, external, primary, or secondary, it is external information, obtained from the company's marketplace, that interests us here.

Most manufacturing companies have no formal program to systematically and continuously gather information about industries, customers, prospects, and competitors in their marketplaces. Survival in business depends upon the ability to compete, yet routine collection and analysis of competitive information is not a common activity in most industrial marketing and sales departments.

Marketing research, an activity more commonly pursued, is part of Marketing intelligence and not a substitute for it. Marketing research is the systematic collection and analysis of data related to specific projects that tend to be discrete and nonrepetitive in nature. Marketing intelligence, on the other hand, is broad in scope, and often deals with many subjects and many sources of information at the same time. It is on-going and continuous in nature. The logic of the Marketing intelligence function in a business is that marketplaces with the power to ultimately accept or reject products and services should be continuously monitored by the company that offers them.

Because accurate and timely information updates, as discussed in Chapter 3, have been beyond the capability of manual systems in most manufacturing companies, marketing and sales executives have had to learn to manage without information efficient management requires. Lack of the competitive information discussed in this chapter provides additional evidence that this point is well made.

We have already observed that the massive raw data manipulation capability of the computer makes information updates practical that were once considered impractical. In view of the fact that computer systems have been installed for many years in thousands of manufacturing companies, why is marketing intelligence gathering not more systematically practiced in industrial marketing and sales management?

The answer to that question may be found in another point made earlier in this book. The technician's concept of an MIS tends to ignore the decision priorities of operating managers. More information is not what is needed. Real information is what is needed. To this suggestion, the following should be added: When computer people talk about information, it is likely to be internal information they are discussing.

In the ordinary course of transacting business, data is acquired that may be processed to produce internal information. This data is usually readily available for processing, in some organized form, within the company. Computer systems have been designed to manage such data. External data is not so readily available. External information of the kind we are discussing is not acquired in the ordinary course of transacting business. As a consequence, the continuous collection and analysis of external information about industries, customers, prospects, and competitors in marketplaces is not a subject likely to be addressed by computer people in manufacturing companies.

WORD PROCESSING

Why marketing intelligence gathering is not more formally practiced in industrial marketing and sales management is an interesting subject. It seems clear that marketing and sales managers would make more informed and effective decisions if real information, from both internal and external sources, were available to them. The measurement of attitudes and opinions in the marketplace is surely part of this.

Marketing intelligence gathering, as presented in this chapter, utilizes the word processing capability of the computer and well-designed questionnaires to formalize and ease the task of continuously collecting and analyzing information about marketplaces, and the industries, customers, prospects, and competitors comprising them. How does the computer's word processing capability formalize and ease the marketing intelligence gathering task? What is word processing?

Word processing is a form of data base management involving textual materials. Word processing systems include hardware and software necessary to store textual material in system memory, retrieve selected material for CRT display, edit the material as desired, and print-out textual revisions. Word processing does away with the inefficiency of searching for appropriate paper file copy, and the time-consuming, manual editing and redrafting procedures associated with paper media. Any textual material repeatedly used, in the same form or in slightly different form, with sections that from time to time are taken out or put in is material that can be handled by a word processing system with electronic efficiency.

Formal price, specification, and delivery quotations, regularly submitted to prospective buyers prior to the award of purchase orders, are examples of textual material that might be more efficiently handled by a word processing system. Other examples are price lists, equipment catalogs, and sales literature periodically revised. There are many more examples. Prominently included among them are mailing lists, cover letters, questionnaires, and the tabulation of questionnaire responses. These represent some of the tools of marketing intelligence gathering.

A typical multiproduct manufacturing company has thousands of customers and prospects. Among the thousands of customers and prospects are more thousands of potential questionnaire recipients. It is not difficult to understand how, in pre-computer days, the burden of handling large amounts of detail manually may have discouraged formal efforts to gather marketing intelligence. The efficiency introduced by the computer's word processing capability encourages marketing intelligence gathering on a systematic and continuous basis.

THE PRINCIPLE OF SELECTIVITY

The primary sources of external information for industrial marketing and sales management are:

1. Total customers: Purchase and use contacts.
2. Customers by market segment: Purchase and use contacts.
3. Total prospects: Purchase and use contacts.
4. Prospects by market segment: Purchase and use contacts.
5. Distributors, reps, and other field sales personnel.

If industrial marketing and sales managers will employ methods outlined in Chapter 7, *The Care and Feeding of the Customer List*, all customers will be identified by four-digit SIC numbers and "establishment size" codes, and a large number of prospects will be identified in the same manner. The identifications will include street address, city, zip code, county, state, and purchase and use contacts.

Effectively, then, the care and feeding of the customer list produces a large but finite population of customers and prospects. This large, finite population may be considered a company's marketing universe. The function of marketing intelligence gathering is to formally provide external information, useful to marketing and sales managers in the process of decision-making, by questioning purchase and use contacts, and field sales personnel, in the marketing universe.

It must be remembered by those involved in questionnaire design that there is such a thing as too much information. Information that does not tell us something of importance we do not already know is not real information. It is noise, and it may obscure really significant facts. The principle of selectivity is an inherent part of any search for information. The attempt to randomly collect all kinds of information from all possible sources is a mistake. Information unrelated to specific objectives in the marketing plan is unlikely to contribute to effective decision-making by marketing and sales managers.

As with any research project, marketing intelligence gathering should begin with a review of problems that may be solved with the help of external information. What kind of information is needed?

Why is it needed? Where may it be obtained? Value analysis discussed in Chapter 3, and the 80/20 rule mentioned in Chapter 5, are examples of the principle of selectivity in action, and are useful guidelines to successful marketing intelligence gathering.

QUESTIONNAIRE DESIGN AND TABULATION

Marketing intelligence gathering may be conducted by personal interview, telephone interview, or mail. In all cases, a formal questionnaire is required for systematic collection and analysis of responses to questions asked. Questionnaire design is not difficult, but consistently good questionnaire design demands that a few rules are observed.

Potential bias is an important consideration in questionnaire design. Bias may be introduced by the way a question is asked. Questionnaires may be designed to record respondent replies that express fact, intention, attitude, reasons why, awareness, and opinion. Good questionnaire design takes these reply categories into consideration. The nature of the reply sought affects the way a question is written, and the way a question is written affects the process of tabulating, analyzing, and interpreting responses.

Bias may be introduced by the choice of respondents asked to reply to questions. If *The Product Acceptance Questionnaire,* one of ten sample questionnaires included in this chapter, were mailed exclusively to a company's good customers, answers to questions asked would likely be biased in favor of the company. Once decisions are made regarding the kind of information needed, why it is needed, and where it may be obtained, good questionnaire design is for the most part an exercise in common sense.

In general, each mailed questionnaire should be accompanied by a short cover letter explaining the reasons for the questionnaire, and asking for the favor of a response. A stamped, self-addressed, envelope should be enclosed for the reply. Do not ask any more questions than you would be willing to answer yourself.

Some reference key should be employed to identify the study, date, industry contacted, SIC and "establishment size," or respondent. There is nothing absolute in this. The system selected should mainly serve the company's identification requirements.

SAMPLE QUESTIONNAIRES

Of ten sample questionnaires, seven are intended for customers and prospects, and three are directed to sales representatives and other field sales personnel.

The Product Performance Questionnaire could be mailed to all customers, customers by market segment, or FYTD customers, in total or by market segment. Nonresponses are followed up by field sales representatives.

The Service Questionnaire could be mailed to customer names and addresses in the service and repair log. In this case, nonresponses are followed up by telephone calls from the home office.

The Salesperson's Performance Questionnaire could be mailed to all customers and prospects, or customers and prospects by market segment. Reference keying customer or prospect purchase and use contacts would be an essential part of the survey. *The Product Acceptance Questionnaire* and *The Product Recognition Questionnaire* could be used in similar surveys.

The Product Application Questionnaire and *The Purchasing Plans Questionnaire* are examples of questionnaires that could be mailed to prospects, in total, or by market segment. Nonresponses are followed up by field sales representatives.

In the ten sample questionnaires presented in this chapter there is a total of fifty-four questions. Between the customers, prospects, and field sales personnel in a typical manufacturing company, these fifty-four questions alone would elicit tens of thousands of replies. The possibilities of developing important, new information in this manner are impressive.

As in questionnaire design, the tabulation of responses is mostly common sense. A last example of bias that can distort and complicate the mailed question survey is the unanswered question. Although the interpretation of unmarked replies is a burden of the mailed questionnaire that will never be entirely eliminated, the problem in general is not a large one.

For companies with heavy statistical demands in marketing intelligence gathering, there is even a way to arrange for the computer to do the tabulating of questionnaire responses. This is called Optical Character Recognition (OCR), and will be discussed in Chapter 10. As with the MAPs discussed in Chapter 8, each sample questionnaire is presented with commentary on the facing page.

SAMPLE QUESTIONNAIRES

PRODUCT PERFORMANCE QUESTIONNAIRE
Commentary

The maintenance characteristics of a particular product, compared to competitive products and compared to all products, might be expected to vary from application to application, and from one market segment to the next.

Answers to questions 3 and 4 on the *Product Performance Questionnaire* would confirm not only the validity of that expectation, but whether or not product maintenance characteristics remained consistent over time, or were improved as a consequence of, perhaps, a change in design.

Given the diversity of product use in large national and international markets, the chances of a product's maintenance characteristics being equally acceptable in all applications is remote.

Success in ordering replacement parts can also vary from market segment to market segment, as well as in terms of a customer's geographical location.

Directing this questionnaire to customer purchase and use contacts makes it possible for manufacturers to learn, firsthand, critical information that would ordinarily reach them secondhand, usually after at least some damage to their reputation has occurred.

PRODUCT PERFORMANCE QUESTIONNAIRE

1. Does the product perform satisfactorily?

   ____YES ____NO ____OTHER

2. Was delivery satisfactory?

   ____YES ____NO ____OTHER

3. How would you rate the maintenance characteristics of the product compared to competitive products?

   ____HIGH ____LOW ____AVERAGE

4. How would you rate the maintenance characteristics of the product compared to all products

   ____HIGH ____LOW ____AVERAGE

5. Have you had difficulty ordering replacement parts?

   ____YES ____NO ____OTHER

6. How does the performance of the product you purchased from us compare with competitive products?

   ____BETTER ____SAME
   ____WORSE ____DON'T KNOW

7. Would you recommend our product to someone else?

   ____YES ____NO ____OTHER

SERVICE QUESTIONNAIRE

Commentary

Because this questionnaire is sent to names and addresses in the service and repair log, there is excellent chance that an important source of information, additional to purchase and use contacts in the customer file, will be uncovered.

Many companies operate their own service departments, returning equipment to the manufacturer only when absolutely necessary. The people who service and repair equipment in plant are an often ignored source of vital information about a manufacturer's products and sales/service capability.

Manufacturers selling products through industrial distributors or manufacturers' representatives would find information contained in answers to questions 3 and 7 particularly useful.

SERVICE
QUESTIONNAIRE

1. Which parts require replacement or repair most often with our equipment?

2. Does our parts department deliver replacement parts satisfactorily?

   ____YES   ____NO   ____OTHER

3. Do you have a current parts list catalog for our products?

   ____YES   ____NO   ____OTHER

4. When did our sales/service representative last call on you?

5. How often do you see our sales/service representative?

   ____EVERY MONTH   ____EVERY THREE MONTHS
   ____OTHER

6. Do you have emergency phone numbers to call for night and weekend service?

   ____YES   ____NO

7. Is our operating manual complete and accurate?

   ____YES   ____NO   ____OTHER

8. How can we improve service on our equipment?

SALESPERSON'S PERFORMANCE QUESTIONNAIRE

Commentary

This questionnaire is directed to a company's customers and prospects in total, or by market segment. Although industrial marketing and sales managers may believe they already possess such information from the point of view of the company's good customers, it is highly unlikely that their confidence extends equally to all customers or all prospects.

It must be remembered also that purchase and use contacts appearing as attributes in the customer file, as discussed in Chapter 7, are often different names and addresses.

Prospect purchase contacts may be favorably impressed by the caliber of a manufacturer's sales representative. That endorsement may not be shared by prospect use contacts, which may explain why the prospect has not become a customer.

SALESPERSON'S PERFORMANCE QUESTIONNAIRE

1. How often does our sales representative call on you?

2. Is our sales representative the caliber of salesperson you would wish to represent your firm?

   ____YES   ____NO   ____OTHER

3. How does our sales representative rate compared to sales representatives selling competitive products?

   ____BETTER   ____SAME   ____WORSE

4. In what areas can our sales representative improve?

PRODUCT ACCEPTANCE QUESTIONNAIRE

Commentary

This questionnaire is sent to customer and prospect purchase and use contacts. Because the likelihood is high that answers to these questions will be greatly variable, the reference keying suggested on page 135 is essential if results of the survey are to be correctly interpreted.

Questions 2 and 5 are questions any marketing and sales manager would like to ask a great number of prospects. The comparison of answers by market segment, SIC and "establishment size," and geographical location would provide important, otherwise unavailable, information to these managers.

Questions 3 and 5 might elicit an occasional reply representing useful insight into a product's marketing future. For lack of a proper forum, products are too often designed without enough consultation with those people who will purchase and use them.

PRODUCT ACCEPTANCE QUESTIONNAIRE

1. Are our prices competitive?

   ____YES   ____NO   ____OTHER

2. Which manufacturers are our strongest competitors?

3. Have our products kept pace with technology?

   ____YES   ____NO   ____OTHER

4. Which competitive firm is most preferred? Why?

5. How would you recommend we improve our products?

PRODUCT APPLICATION QUESTIONNAIRE

Commentary

This questionnaire can be used as one way of systematically qualifying any number of prospects identified by methods discussed in
Chapter 7. Eliminating prospects who are really not prospects,
and qualifying long-term and short-term prospects, are important
contingent parts of the exercises described in that chapter.

Identifying the prospect purchase contact is usually easier than
identifying the prospect use contact. Assuming this questionnaire
is mailed to the former, question 5 helps with the latter.

PRODUCT APPLICATION
QUESTIONNAIRE

1. Do you presently have a specific application for our product?

   ____YES   ____NO   ____OTHER

2. Are you presently using a competitive product for this application?

   ____YES   ____NO   ____OTHER

3. Do you have future applications planned for which our product could serve your needs?

   ____YES   ____NO   ____OTHER

4. What engineering or design changes would make our product more suitable for your needs?

5. Who is the person at the plant level with authority to specify our type of product?

PRODUCT RECOGNITION QUESTIONNAIRE

Commentary

This questionnaire is mailed to customers and prospects in total, or by market segment. Advertising expenditures in many manufacturing companies are high cost expenditures. In view of this fact, it is remarkable how many advertisers rely on advertising agencies and trade magazines to provide the information associated with answers to these questions. Despite the respectability and integrity of most of the firms involved, the conflict of interest would be questioned by manufacturers in other contexts.

In the pre-computer past, of course, a manufacturing company would have been less inclined to develop and coordinate such a survey.

PRODUCT RECOGNITION QUESTIONNAIRE

1. What brand first comes to mind when you think about products such as ours?

2. What brand of this product type is advertised most?

3. Which type of advertising does the best job of drawing your attention to these products?

   _____ Trade journals   _____ Equipment catalogs
   _____ Direct mail   _____ Other
   _____ Trade shows

4. What features do you associate most prominently with products such as ours?

   _____ Design   _____ Performance
   _____ Price   _____ Quality
   _____ Appearance _____ Size

5. Was price a significant factor when you last purchased such a product?

   ____YES   ____NO   ____OTHER

PURCHASING PLANS QUESTIONNAIRE

Commentary

This questionnaire is mailed to prospects in total, or by market segment. Capital goods acquisition follows in many industries a budget set months in advance of the purchase award.

This would be a timely survey if sent to prospect purchase contacts after budgets for the coming operating period were established. This questionnaire supplements information ordinarily supplied exclusively by sales representatives.

PURCHASING PLANS
QUESTIONNAIRE

1. Is your company now contemplating the purchase of any of the following kinds of equipment?

	YES	NO	DON'T KNOW
a.	____	____	____
b.	____	____	____
c.	____	____	____

2. If so, how many units will be involved?

3. Who has primary responsibility for specifying this equipment?

4. Is our company on the bidder's list for this equipment?

5. If not, who do we contact in your company in order to be placed on the bidder's list for this equipment?

MANUFACTURERS' REPRESENTATIVE
QUESTIONNAIRE
Commentary

A manufacturer selling products through a handful of manufacturers' representatives would probably not use this questionnaire. But manufacturers who have many manufacturers' representatives in widely dispersed geographical locations would find this survey useful from time to time.

The questionnaire is most informative when mailed to individual salespeople rather than exclusively to the management of the rep firm.

MANUFACTURERS' REPRESENTATIVE QUESTIONNAIRE

1. Are you kept adequately supplied with current price lists, equipment catalogs, technical bulletins, and sales literature?

   ____YES   ____NO   ____OTHER

2. How do sales of your major lines this year compare with last year at this time? (*approximate percent)

   ABOVE____   SAME____   BELOW____

3. What can we do to help you improve sales of our products?

4. Do we return your telephone calls promptly?

   ____YES   ____NO   ____OTHER

5. Do we answer your correspondence promptly?

   ____YES   ____NO   ____OTHER

6. With regard to the future sales of our products, what would you like to see us do that we are not doing now?

MARKET SHARE QUESTIONNAIRE

Commentary

This questionnaire is self-explanatory. It is most informative when mailed to individual salespersons rather than exclusively to the management of a rep or distributor firm.

MARKET SHARE
QUESTIONNAIRE

1. Are we getting a satisfactory share of the expanding markets for our products in your area?

   ____YES   ____NO

   Explain:

2. Are any of our products close to saturation in market segments in your area?

   ____YES   ____NO

   Explain:

3. Are we overlooking profitable market segments in your area?

   ____YES   ____NO

   Explain:

4. In the past year, is our share of the total market for our products in your area,

   ____UP?   ____SAME?   ____DOWN?

   Explain:

PRODUCT REDESIGN QUESTIONNAIRE

Commentary

This questionnaire is sent to industrial distributors, reps, and other field sales personnel. The questions in this survey should be regarded as supplemental to information supplied by these representatives and managers in the ordinary course of business. Such information, despite its great value from time to time, is casual.

This survey represents a systematic attempt to gather product redesign information from an important source.

PRODUCT REDESIGN QUESTIONNAIRE

1. Is there a change in users' needs that will affect the way our products are designed?

   ____YES   ____NO

   Explain:

2. What competitive design features are superior to ours?

3. Have any customers or prospects mentioned design changes that are being made by competitors?

   ____YES   ____NO

   Explain:

4. Have any customers or prospects indicated that they would like to see design changes in our products?

   ____YES   ____NO

   Explain:

5. Which action would be more likely to improve sales in your area?

   ____Product redesign   ____Price reduction

PART FIVE

A LOOK AT THE FUTURE IN INDUSTRIAL MARKETING AND SALES MANAGEMENT

PLUG-IN MARKETING PRODUCTIVITY

The Introduction to this book mentioned that the marketing and sales manager who remains unimpressed by the inevitability of the computer in industrial marketing and sales management applications is working on borrowed time. As we have discussed many times and in many ways throughout the first nine chapters, there are a great number of industrial marketing and sales management routines that can be rationalized with the help of the computer. Increased operating efficiency and improved marketing productivity are predictable results.

In this brief concluding chapter, we discuss the electronic office of the future in terms of marketing productivity. Because the paperless office depends upon computer systems, advanced electronic packages, and telemetering techniques, many of which are designed for turnkey installation, this chapter is entitled *Plug-In Marketing Productivity*.

COMPUTERS AND TIME MANAGEMENT

It has already been said that, to most industrial marketing and sales managers, the long roads are the only roads. There is no better illustration than the way managers spend time during a typical workday. It is fair to say that on the average day most operating managers, including marketing and sales managers, devote less than two hours to the analytical considerations and the thoughtful deliberation that informed decision-making demands. Valuable management time is squandered in the following nonmanagerial activities:

1. Searching for documents in files
2. Searching for pertinent information in a document after it has been located in a file
3. Trying to contact other people, either by dialing a telephone number or by visiting a nearby office
4. Scheduling and rescheduling meetings
5. Attending unnecessary meetings (Fire-fighting exercises are often a substitute for information that would have helped avoid the crisis in the first place.)
6. Traveling to distant cities to attend business meetings.

The fact that valuable management time is lost to avoidable busywork is not difficult to establish. But when everyone is wasting management time in the same way, the long roads *can* seem to be the only roads. In this light, convincing marketing and sales managers that increased operating efficiency and improved marketing productivity may require changes in the way they have spent their workdays (perhaps for many years) cannot be expected to be easy. Nevertheless, here are some of the ways plug-in marketing productivity will be accomplished in industrial marketing and sales management:

1. *Information retrieval.* On-line information retrieval made possible by the computer has been discussed throughout this book. The marketing application programs (MAPs) discussed in Chapter 8 represent a source of internal information retrieval. Marketing intelligence gathering discussed in Chapter 9 is an important source of external information retrieval.

Industrial marketing and sales managers, using desk top computers and modems, are also able to plug-in by telephone to many large data banks located all over the world—another important source of external information retrieval. In recent years, hundreds of computer data banks and information retrieval services have emerged, reducing time spent searching for collected information from days to minutes. Here are a few examples of what is presently available:

    a.   There are data banks that summarize major business articles that have been published in the past five years.

b. There are data banks that supply information about overseas markets, foreign suppliers, and competitive importers.

c. There are data banks that list the number of books and articles published on a particular subject.

d. There are data banks that supply competitive information about publicly held companies.

e. There are data banks that supply competitive information about privately held companies.

f. There are data banks that provide updated information on industrial, and consumer, markets.

g. There are computerized services that specialize in economic forecasting, and allow the user to perform his or her own sales correlation calculations using data stored in files.

The list of external data banks accessible to the computer is long, and becoming longer. They represent many sources of vital information for managers, and make it possible for all competitors in an industry to utilize information once available only to the largest companies.

2. *Information transfer.* Managers spend much of their time transferring information by telephone. But there is an important distinction that should be made between information transfer and information discussion. Because the distinction is not made, valuable management time is wasted.

Unlike interactive information discussion, information transfer does not require simultaneous consideration by the sender and the recipient. The sender of information to be transferred can more efficiently transmit the information if the business of having to first arrange personal telephone contact with the receiver is eliminated. The receiver of information that was transferred can more efficiently review the information at a time of his or her own choosing, without having to interrupt another activity in order to respond to an often unexpected telephone call.

A number of systems have been introduced to transfer information more conveniently, and in some cases less expensively, than traditional telephone and mail systems. Micro-processor controlled telephones, and an array of electronic mail devices, make possible:

a. high-speed transmission of digital data by radio, satellite, cable, or any transmission medium carrying digital signals

b. facsimile transmission over telephone lines of hard copy image documents

By using desk top input/output devices, managers are able to send and receive simple and common forms of communication when it is convenient. They may also electronically originate, edit, and review documents such as charts, blueprints, and drawings. They can write, and send hand-drawn forms over the telephone. They can even record speech in message forms that can be transmitted immediately, and stored for hearing by a listener at a convenient time.

Electronic mail relieves managers from the time-wasting frustration of busy signals, missed telephone calls, the inevitable delays associated with telephone calling, and mail delays. It is commonly predicted that electronic mail will be used in years to come as conventionally as standard telephone and mail systems are used today.

3. *Teleconferencing.* Millions of dollars are wasted annually by industry in unnecessary business travel. It is anticipated that technology will eventually make available a commonly affordable "fast scan" TV image that can be broadcast for teleconferencing. Teleconferences make possible face-to-face meetings over long distances without travel. In addition, teleconferencing allows the number of participants in a meeting to be as large or small as required. Replay capability also makes possible a reliable documentation of what was said and agreed upon during the course of the meeting.

4. *Activity management.* There are many examples of how the computer can be used to more efficiently control and communicate the activities of people involved in the management of a company. Schedule conflicts would be immediately apparent if the scheduler of a meeting were able to review a participant's calendar, on a CRT screen, before the meeting was announced.

The maintenance of a master time schedule for all managers is another example of the way the computer can be used to more efficiently schedule and reschedule meetings, and control and communicate the activities of managers.

5. *Project and task management.* The computer can be programmed to generate task reminder "needles" automatically, at periodic intervals, until notification that a particular task has been completed. In this sense, the computer becomes the electronic equivalent of a "tickle" file system, with the potential for relieving the management frustration associated with unintentionally missed commitment dates.

For industrial marketing and sales management purposes, the computer can also be programmed to generate reminder "needles" regarding large purchase projects. In many manufacturing companies purchase projects are global, often involving more than one purchase influence in more than one country. The time horizon, from project inception to purchase order awards, can span many years. It is not unusual for companies to find themselves "spec'd out" of large purchase projects because they were unable to precisely track project progress.

    6.   *Optical Character Recognition (OCR) devices.*   An optical character recognition device can be employed to read data from business documents when input volume is large; hence, computer terminals become expensive typewriters. In the OCR, a laser beam scans hand-fed or automatically-fed documents. The beam "reads" light and dark images, translates the image field into digital data, and feeds the data into storage.

Most OCR devices presently read typed documents, but some have already been designed to read typeset, printed, or photocopied material. A well-designed OCR system will presently handle up to 300 pages of material per hour. Manufacturers of OCR reading equipment design it for plug-in compatibility with most existing computer systems.

    7.   *Full-color graphic displays.*   Managers often find a picture worth ten thousand rows and columns of data. Fortunately, the conversion of hard-to-interpret data print-outs into more easily understood full-color graphic displays is a common computer programming technique commercially available in plug-in electronic packages. A color graphics terminal utilizes electronic color-producing "guns," together with a grid specification on the CRT screen, in order to visually represent data.

Reference points within the grid are located by the user on the surface of the CRT screen. A light pen, consisting of flexible lines that correspond to reference points, may be employed to touch locations on the grid. The location of a point touched on the screen surface is sensed by the pen, and a grid coordinate is communicated to the computer in the form of a digital signal. Touching a number of reference points creates 'pictures' in the shape of line graphs, charts, and histograms which visually represent the data entered into the computer by the light pen.

    8.   *Voice input/output.*   Most business executives are unskilled and unwilling typists. That fact has been recognized as an obstacle to wide acceptance of the electronic office.

While many executives may be uncomfortable communicating with the computer by typewriter, all executives talk. Intelligent terminals have been developed that make it possible to enter data into the computer by voiced commands. Using a voice-operated terminal, the reluctant manager-typist is able to tell a computer what to do.

THE CHALLENGE OF THE FORMAL, DECISION-ORIENTED, SYSTEM

Most industrial marketing and sales managers respond vigorously to challenge. This concluding chapter has summarized a number of ways managers can plug-in to marketing productivity. These are, of course, additional to materials presented in earlier chapters wherein steps to be taken in the development of a formal, decision-oriented, computer-based information system in marketing and sales management were discussed in considerable detail. As this book comes to a close, it is fitting to suggest that the greatest challenge to the implementation of such a system may lie in the requirement that human behavior be modified; a topic beyond the scope of this book and the competence of the author.

It was earlier said that our principle objective in these pages has been to emphasize the desirability of a formal, decision-oriented, information system in the order-getting activities in industrial marketing and sales management, acknowledging that the rationalization of order-filling activities has been favorably influenced already by MRP-based scheduling techniques in production and inventory management. It was also stated that something less than a profound rationalization of industrial marketing and sales management routines might be all that can be expected from these pioneer efforts.

Despite the modesty of our intentions and claims, the requirement that industrial marketing and sales managers be willing not only to learn to think differently about what they are trying to accomplish but, to alter their work habits and the way they spend time, represents a great challenge to them.

Computer technology is neutral. The people who choose to employ or ignore the computer are not neutral. Industrial marketing and sales managers must be responsible for the information systems they develop, and this is perhaps the greatest challenge of all.

BIBLIOGRAPHY

The subjects of management are many, but the craft primarily involves effective decision-making capability and skills. This book is about using the computer to improve the industrial marketing and sales management craft and marketing productivity. As there is at present a modest literature about this subject, this is a brief bibliography pointing out a few books and articles of interest to the student and executive.

COMPUTER SYSTEMS

Didday, R. *Home Computers: Volume 1 and 2.* P.O. Box 92, Forest Grove, Oregon: Dilithium Press, 1977.
 For anyone interested in learning about the technicalities of how computers work, these question and answer texts are excellent self-teaching tools. Volume 1 tackles the hardware subject. Volume 2 discusses software.
Orlicky, J. A. *The Successful Computer System.* New York: McGraw-Hill, 1969.
 This book is easy to read and provides a basic understanding of what is required in order to plan, develop, and manage a successful computer-based system in business enterprise.
Sanders, N. *A Manager's Guide to Profitable Computers.* New York: Amacom, 1978.
 Written tongue-in-cheek, this book is both entertaining and informative. Mr. Sanders knows his subject, pointing out the common pitfalls associated with making computers work in business.

COMPUTER-BASED INFORMATION SYSTEMS

Ackoff, R. L. "Management Misinformation Systems." *Management Science* (December 1967).

Subject: Five common, often unjustified, assumptions commonly made by designers of MIS's.

King, W., and Cleland, D. "Environmental Information Systems for Strategic Marketing Planning." *Journal of Marketing* (October 1974).

Subject: An information system for providing externally generated data to support strategic marketing planning.

Kirk, F. *Total System Development For Information Systems.* New York: Wiley-Interscience, 1973.

This book describes in great detail the process of developing computer-based man-machine information systems.

Stasch, S. F. *Systems Analysis For Marketing Planning And Control.* Glenview, Illinois: Scott, Foresman and Company, 1972.

This book takes a quantitative approach to systems analysis concepts as applied to marketing and sales management. It is not light reading, but in particular succeeds in outlining the questions marketing and sales managers must answer before determining how the appropriate data should be processed for decision-making purposes.

MARKETING PRODUCTIVITY

Sevin, C. *Marketing Productivity Analysis.* New York: McGraw-Hill, 1965.

Those interested in a detailed presentation of the analytical requirements associated with the improvement of marketing productivity will find this book useful.

INDEX

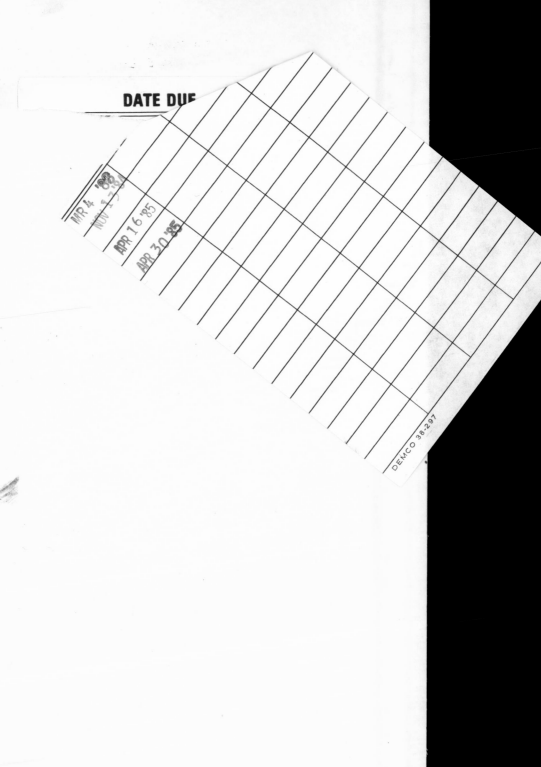